ENABLING CHURCH

ENABLING CHURCH

A Bible-based resource towards the full inclusion of disabled people

GORDON TEMPLE with LIN BALL

First published in Great Britain in 2012

Society for Promoting Christian Knowledge
36 Causton Street
London SW1P 4ST
www.spckpublishing.co.uk

The authors and publisher have made every effort to ensure that the external website
and email addresses included in this book are correct and up to date at the time
of going to press. The authors and publisher are not responsible for the content,
quality or continuing accessibility of the sites.

The publisher and authors acknowledge with thanks permission to reproduce
extracts from the following:
'Goodness is stronger than evil': from *Love & Anger* (Wild Goose Publications,
1997). Words & Music John L. Bell, Copyright © 1997 WGRG, Iona Community,
Glasgow G2 3DH, Scotland. Reproduced by permission. www.wgrg.co.uk
Every effort has been made to seek permission to use copyright material reproduced in
this book. The publisher apologizes for those cases where permission might not have
been sought and, if notified, will formally seek permission at the earliest opportunity.

British Library Cataloguing-in-Publication Data
A catalogue record for this book is available from the British Library

ISBN 978–0–281–06649–0
eBook ISBN 978–0–281–06650–6

Typeset by Graphicraft Ltd, Hong Kong
First printed in Great Britain by Ashford Colour Press
Subsequently digitally printed in Great Britain

Produced on paper from sustainable forests

Contents

Foreword

One of the things I welcome about this creative and timely book is its confidence that Scripture is the starting point for thinking about disability. For some decades activists and academics have been debating disability issues, often expressing radical and new ideas. Yet the Church has taken some time to catch on to the idea that some of our perspectives on disability are being challenged. Words like 'charity' are now seen as inappropriate and are being replaced with the concepts of 'rights' and 'justice'. The idea of doing something 'for' disabled people is being replaced by disabled people doing things for themselves in partnership with others, wherever possible.

The idea that disability is a deficiency in the body – a deviation from normality – has been challenged by the recognition that the word 'disabled' is also a verb. People with impairments are 'being disabled' by societal attitudes as well as through lack of access to its infrastructure. The slogan of the disability movement, 'nothing about us without us', shows the extent to which things have changed – and rightly so. Yet we also still need to draw on best practice in healthcare and healing.

By the time the Church became involved in the debate there were already models, perspective and ideologies in vogue which seemed, in turn, either attractive to or in disagreement with a Christian worldview. All of them had both strengths and weaknesses. Nevertheless, it was too easy for Christians involved in the disability debate to start with these models, despite the fact that none of them was adequate to represent a Christian perspective.

It is not that we do not have a great deal to learn from the perspectives of others; we do. But if we do not believe that Scripture should be our starting point for thinking about any of the great issues of the day we are in danger of losing both our distinctiveness and our authority.

The starting point, as John Naudé points out in his Introduction, is the statement which stands at the heart of the creation story that humankind is made in the image of God. Yet we cannot go back to Eden. We can only know what it means to be made in the image of God by basing our thinking on Christ who 'is the image of the invisible God'. Christian thinking about disability is focused on Christ.

Jesus shows us what it means to be a human being. He loves those who are marginalized and has a costly passion for justice. He shows us that though suffering is something which even he, in Gethsemane, wished to avoid, it can be used by God to demonstrate his purposes for the world. He also shows us that we live in the certain hope of a new world coming where we shall all, whatever our bodies are like, be transformed in order to live in a world where there is no suffering and in which it is impossible to displease God.

In emulating Christ we learn what it is, both in our personal lives and in the life of the Church, to be people who love justice, fight alongside those who have been denied their rights and work to bring about inclusive relationships in the community. We long to be the diverse Church of which Jesus spoke, and about which others comment, 'See how they love one another'.

Roy McCloughry

Acknowledgements:
Enabling Church

We acknowledge our indebtedness to the speaking team from the very first 'Enabling Church' conference held in October 2010 in London, organized by Churches for All – a partnership of Christian disability organizations – and sponsored by Premier Christian Radio. Their contributions at this milestone event were the inspiration for this resource.

Introduction

Enabling is what I believe the Church should be about: enabling all people to discover God's amazing love; and enabling each person in the body of Christ to play his or her part, so the Church of Christ can function to its full potential.

Sadly, the Church has not done this in the past. But it is moving forward, especially in the way it sees the ministry, gifting and needs of disabled people. Historically, disabled people have been perceived as people 'we minister to' or as 'pew fodder', not as people who are integral to Christ's Church.

The 'Enabling Church' conference in London 2010 was an amazing event in which God brought together the speakers under one uniting banner: simply this, that disabled people are people made in the image of God. While this may seem a rather basic message, the implications are immense.

The way we value people for who they are, as they are, is so important. Disabled people still often receive the message that their disability is as a result of their sin or the sin of their parents. When we fail to see an individual with a disability as being made in the image of God, we can apply hidden pressure that he or she needs to conform to what is 'normal' in our society. This is heard so many times in the stories of disabled people who have been pressured to be healed, or who say that when God does not appear to heal it is assumed to be their fault. Perhaps they do not have enough faith or are holding on to some unconfessed sin. This has left some disabled people damaged in the way they see themselves and the way they see God.

However, as I say, the Church is changing! The publication of this book is yet another step forward. It is an excellent resource for those who want to discover more about enabling the Church to include disabled people. It helps an individual or group grow deeper in their understanding of disability and, more importantly, form a godly perspective on those with a disability.

This is an accessible book in so many ways. The teaching is clear, biblical and engaging. The authors have used creative material to help us go deeper in our understanding, allowing us to see others and ourselves as part of God's beautiful creation – each and every individual made in God's image.

John Naudé

Author's introduction:
Living interdependently

The life experience of those in the African bush is so different from that of those in Europe, as I discovered on a trip to Malawi and Uganda. I felt privileged to spend time with some of the poorest people on the planet: blind people living in remote villages, people with nothing but a few clothes, no cash and no certainty of a next meal. What struck me most, as I absorbed the painfully stark realities of African life, was the dignity of those with a living relationship with Jesus as their Saviour and Lord.

We are all made in the image of God. This is a fundamental truth, equally valid for European or African, disabled or not; although the question of whether any of us is truly 'non-disabled' and, if we are, whether that endures for more than a season, is up for discussion. Our understanding that we are all made in God's image is the soil in which the dignity of humanity is rooted; not in our own achievements, nor in the approval of others – but in a relationship with our Creator God.

Some of us need to hear this afresh. The Psalmist expresses it beautifully. We are 'fearfully and wonderfully made', he says (Psalm 139.14). This is how God sees each one of us. He made us and loves us unconditionally. It makes no difference if we are young or old; if we see or don't see; if we walk or don't walk; if we hear or don't hear; if we speak or don't speak. It's of no consequence to God's love if we feel humiliated by epileptic seizures or are disfigured by the loss of a limb, or even if we can't remember our own name because of the ravages of dementia. Our learning disability may mean our response to his love is no more than a smile. It makes no difference. God made us and loves us, each one special and beautiful.

The biblical truth that we – every one of us – are made in the image of God was the starting point for a conference held in London in October 2010 called 'Enabling Church – Christian theology, disability and wholeness'. I had the privilege of leading the planning of this event. It was a remarkable occasion at which almost 500 got together to think, talk and pray about the theology of disability. It was remarkable in another sense too. As speaker followed speaker, there emerged a pattern of thought that, in the view of many, cemented some important biblically rooted insights into an emerging model of disability.

Models of disability – ways of thinking about disability – have evolved and continue to evolve. They are important because they are used in shaping social policies and political agendas.

The **medical model** has been defined largely in retrospect to reflect what was actually happening before disability rights initiatives challenged long-held assumptions. In the medical model view, disabled people need either fixing (treatment) or care. This fits comfortably with the Christian virtue of compassion, but the risk is that disabled people are disempowered, made dependent and lose dignity. Others make decisions about their lives from positions of expertise and power. Sadly, in the past this has had the consequence that disabled people were put into institutions and forgotten – and this still happens in some countries.

The **social model** views so-called disabled people as those having impairments who find themselves *dis*-abled by barriers presented by social structures, the built environment and prejudiced attitudes. This model aims to give disabled people access, independence and dignity – and to put them in control of any care and support they may need to live a fulfilling life. Of course, Christians can identify with this too, as we assert the fundamental dignity of any human being by virtue of being made in the image of God.

But this, I believe, is not the end of the story. To some extent the social model is defined in opposition to the medical model, and herein lies a danger. As 'Enabling Church' conference contributor Roy McCloughry pointed out to delegates, he lives with both models simultaneously: he welcomes the expert-led medical intervention that aims to regulate his epilepsy, but equally wishes to make choices without restriction related to his disability.

In Genesis 1.26 we read, 'Then God said, "Let us make humankind in our image, according to our likeness".' The God who made us in his image is plural: Father, Son and Holy Spirit. Being imprinted with the image of God includes the divine characteristic of community. We don't function at our best when alone. We are made for relationship, designed and built for companionship and community. It's in our DNA!

Here, a word of caution. Like so many terms, 'community' is a word that has been devalued, particularly by its use in political and public policy. As a result, some disabled people have negative associations with this word. One disabled person said to me during the writing of this book: 'The *big society* seems to be a sort of abandonment without funding.' Yet, properly used, 'community' captures vital truths about relationships for all of us, throughout our lives.

The consumerist culture of the West that seems to be spreading unchecked across the globe fosters individualism and selfishness that works in opposition to that idea of community. The aim of bringing independence to those who live with disability has driven much that is good and helpful, and is to be celebrated. But there's a danger of going too far in the pursuit of independence, with the perverse consequence that disabled people can become all the more isolated and lonely. There are times when we all need the help of those around us. This is not about weakness or failure, but about complementarity and community, about how things should be.

*The Bible affirms the dignity of all people and supports neither a strident, heroic **independency** nor an abject, passive **dependency** – but gives us wholesome pictures of **interdependency**. The gospel is intrinsically relational. As we are drawn into a relationship with our Creator we are drawn towards one another.*

No one can 'go it alone'. We need each other. 'No one is indispensable' is usually said to those who bother us by their self-importance. But in the Church *everyone is indispensable.* God has gifted each to contribute in a diversity of ways, and it's tragic when the only response of the Church to disabled people is the provision of compassion and care. Disabled people may well need the help and support of others on occasion, but that's not the end of the story.

Within the kingdom of God there's a place of significance for every one of us. We are all made in God's image, and through new birth into God's kingdom that image is being restored in us. We are imprinted with the image of a God who himself lives in community and models relationship in perfection, and he calls us to foster kingdom relationships that aspire to that quality. Only together can we be the authentic Church – Christ's body living on earth and engaged in the crucial work of kingdom building.

That's what this resource *Enabling Church*, is about – the search for meaningful and fruitful interdependence between all people that will make churches whole and effective, to the glory of God.

Dr Gordon Temple, CEO, Torch Trust

How to get the best out of this resource

This book is written for any church, home group or individual believing that any disabled person should be welcomed, valued and enabled to make a contribution to the work of God in his or her community. The contributors hope that you will find insights, practical ideas and encouragement – but also a strong biblical mandate for change in attitude and practice.

Although this material has a particular focus on including people who are considered disabled, the principles explored apply to any marginalized group.

Enabling Church provides you with a flexible menu of study materials, stories, personal views, discussion, worship and prayer activities suited for a wide range of churches. Leaders should choose the activities that will be most meaningful to their group and appropriate to the time available. It is not anticipated that any group would try to complete all the activities! You will note that fewer options are included for the first and last sessions. This is to allow time for the group to get to know each other a little in the first session, and to have a wide-ranging discussion in the last session about the application of the principles explored.

Seven sessions are suggested but shorter or longer courses could be constructed from the material. It could be adapted easily to fit a two-day conference, church weekend away or leaders' retreat.

No assumptions are made about levels of understanding of the Bible. The material could be followed by groups with limited or extensive Bible knowledge. Some of the activities are suitable for use in a whole-congregation context.

Considering that the topic under consideration is disability, do ensure that the group is accessible (that is, that there are no obstacles to disabled people attending and participating) and that the offer of alternative formats in which this book is available (Braille, large print, audio) is made to people who may have sight loss.

Given the flexible format of the material, it's recommended that the leader has some experience of leading group discussions. The leadership role should be considered that of guide or facilitator rather than teacher, enabling and encouraging others to contribute. The leader should read the material thoroughly in advance, make an appropriate selection of activities, and ensure that any 'props' or visual aids required are provided. In most cases these are fairly simply obtained – newspapers, pens, flipchart and so on. After the first session or two, consider delegating some sections to others to lead. Sharing responsibility will strengthen the group.

All group members should have a copy of this workbook. When group members commit to reading and thinking about the material in advance, this will prove a real advantage to the ease of conversation. Members should be encouraged to bring along Bibles. Selected verses from the passages are printed but you could choose to read them in full from your own Bibles. Unless otherwise stated, the NRSV (the New Revised Standard Version) is used in this book. It may be helpful to refer to other versions, for example the popular New International Version (NIV). Those new to Bible study may find using the Contemporary English Version (CEV) good; the New Living Translation (NLT) is also recommended.

What would success look like for groups or individuals using this material? It's not about 'right' answers! It's about everyone being on a journey of discovery. If everyone has interacted in a lively and thoughtful way with:

- the Bible passage, and
- each other, free to express themselves and considerately listening to the views of others, and
- God in prayer,

then that's success!

Each section starts with one or more Bible passages, together with comments which will give a context for discussion: the **Bible briefing** and **Bible briefing notes**. This is followed by the **Disability Wall**, quotations from people with personal insights – people who are themselves disabled or closely connected with disabled people. Many of these were speakers at the first 'Enabling Church' conference. After this comes a range of **Discussion questions** and **Taking it further** activities. Depending on your group, you may wish to choose to sing in your session – but do select songs or hymns with values that match the values of the material.

Throughout the book are a number of reports called **Real life,** which allow disabled people to speak for themselves. Use these in the discussion times, or read one sometimes as the group comes to prayer.

Please note the different usages of the words 'Deaf' and 'deaf' in this book. 'Deaf', with a capital 'D', refers to 'culturally deaf' members of the Deaf community, whose first or preferred language is British Sign Language (BSL), and who view themselves primarily as a linguistic-cultural minority. The much larger number of people with a measurable hearing loss, who identify more with the language and culture of the majority hearing society, are referred to as 'deaf', with a small 'd'. These are not labels externally imposed; individuals may decide for themselves which group they belong to.

Quoted on the Disability Wall

Laurence Banks

Laurence Banks is Deaf. He has worked with Go! Sign for over ten years and is currently employed as their part-time ministry director. He preaches and teaches around the UK and overseas and has recently completed a theology degree at the London School of Theology.

Susan Boyle

Susan Boyle is a Scottish singer who came to international attention when she appeared on the reality TV programme *Britain's Got Talent*. Her first album became a number one best-selling CD on charts all over the world.

Bob Brooke

Bob Brooke is a chaplain with people who have learning disabilities.

Alan Chantler

Alan Chantler is a former university lecturer who twice had cancer – the second time it came in a rare form which caused his spine to collapse. His story is told in 'Real life' on page 16.

Jonathan Clark

Jonathan Clark is Director for Premier Life at Premier Christian Radio and a director of Mind and Soul, a non-denominational organization exploring Christianity and mental health. He also runs the Premier Lifeline telephone helpline. He has been a church minister and is a qualified social worker.

Revd Nick Cook

Nick Cook is the minister of a Baptist church in the East Midlands which has a number of blind people in its congregation, several of whom have served in key roles in the church leadership.

Revd Malcolm Duncan

Malcolm Duncan is the founder and director of Church and Community, a charity committed to helping local churches embrace an inclusive and holistic approach to mission. He is a pastor, author, conference speaker and government advisor on issues of faith and identity. He has personal experience of disability in his family life. Since 2010 he has been the lead pastor at Gold Hill Baptist Church.

Professor John Hull

John Hull is a distinguished Christian academic and author who became blind in 1980 in his 40s; he has been responsible for some seminal and hard-hitting thinking on the theology of disability.

Irenaeus

Irenaeus was one of the earliest great Christian theologians, a second-century bishop in Gaul, then part of the Roman Empire. As an early church father, his writings were formative in the development of Christian theology.

Helen Keller

Helen Keller (1880–1968) was an American author and political activist, and the first deafblind person to earn a degree.

Jonathan Lamb

Jonathan Lamb contracted polio at the age of five and has lived with mild disability ever since, which has an impact mainly on his mobility. He has ministered in many parts of the world through his work with the International Fellowship of Evangelical Students and with Langham Partnership International. He has served as a church leader for many years, and is currently chair of Keswick Ministries.

Rt Revd Michael Langrish

Michael Langrish, Bishop of Exeter, began his career in education, including lecturing in Nigeria. After ordination he spent 20 years in a variety of urban and rural parishes. He has been a member of the House of Lords since 2005. He has extensive professional and personal experience of working in disability and social care.

Roy McCloughry

Roy McCloughry lectures in Ethics at St John's College, Nottingham. He is the author of over a dozen books on contemporary social issues including *Making a World of Difference: Christian reflections on disability*, with Wayne Morris (SPCK, 2002). He is chairman of Lion Hudson Publishing and vice-president of Livability. He has had epilepsy all his life.

Neil Marcus

Playwright Neil Marcus has dystonia, a rare neurological disorder in which powerful involuntary muscle spasms twist and jerk the body into unusual postures. Neil has the most severe and painful form of this, which denies the ability to speak, stand, walk or control sudden movements.

Revd John Naudé

John Naudé is chair of Churches for All – a partnership of Christian disability organizations. He is also minister of an Anglican church near Portsmouth, a wheelchair user and athlete.

Tony Phelps-Jones

Tony Phelps-Jones is on the leadership team of Prospects, the leading Christian organization working with people with learning disabilities. Tony is hard of hearing.

Revd David Potter

David Potter and his wife Madeleine founded A Cause for Concern in 1976, renamed Prospects in 1997. David, a former Baptist minister, led the organization for over 20 years. He was awarded an MBE in 2005 for lifelong services to people with learning disabilities.

Revd Dr John Stott OBE

Leading Christian teacher and author of over 50 books, John Stott was listed by *Time* magazine in 2005 as one of the 100 most influential people in the world. He died in 2011.

Joni Eareckson Tada

Joni Eareckson Tada became quadriplegic following a diving accident in her teens. She is a leading disability advocate with the JAF International Disability Center in Southern California. Joni leads a team which holds international family retreats and distributes wheelchairs and Bibles to disabled people and their families in developing nations.

Dr Gordon Temple

Gordon Temple is executive officer of Churches for All and also serves as chief executive of Torch Trust, a role he has had since 2002. Torch seeks to enable people with sight loss to lead fulfilling Christian lives.

Dr Mike Townsend

Mike Townsend is blind, and a trustee and consultant for a number of disability organizations including Torch Trust, RNIB and Guide Dogs. He also chairs Through the Roof.

Jean Vanier

Jean Vanier is a Canadian Catholic philosopher who founded L'Arche, an international organization which creates communities where people with learning disabilities can share their lives with others.

Susan Wendell

Susan Wendell is a feminist writer diagnosed in 1985 with myalgic encephalomyelitis/chronic fatigue syndrome. She is the author of *The Rejected Body: Feminist Philosophical Reflections on Disability* (Routledge, 1996) and other works.

1

Knowing we're made in his image

Genesis 1.26–31; 1 John 3.2

Purpose: to explore what it means to be human, made in God's image; to challenge prejudices about what is 'normal'.

Prayer

- Thank God for the Bible – his inspired message to us all – and for all that it can teach us of God's plan for humanity. Ask that the Holy Spirit will inspire each person in the group with a clear and fresh understanding of its message.

- Pray that each person attending will have an open mind, prepared for the cobwebs of unhelpful thought patterns to be blown away.

Bible briefing

Then God said, 'Let us make humankind in our image . . .'

in the image of God he created them;
male and female he created them.

God blessed them, and God said to them, 'Be fruitful and multiply, and fill the earth and subdue it; and have dominion over the fish of the sea and over the birds of the air and over every living thing that moves upon the earth.'

. . . God saw everything that he had made, and indeed, it was very good.   (Genesis 1.26–31)

13

Beloved, we are God's children now; what we will be has not yet been revealed. What we do know is this: when he is revealed, we will be like him, for we will see him as he is. (1 John 3.2)

Bible briefing notes

The Old Testament assertion that we are made in God's image and the New Testament aspiration that we shall all become like his Son are profound concepts that lie at the heart of our faith.

God's own reflection on creation was that it was 'very good'. We might say that it was perfect. What then are our contemporary ideas about perfection? We celebrate the waif-like Kate Moss as the perfection of physical woman, the footballer David Beckham as the epitome of sporting manhood. So are these two superstars anything like the image of God? Are they more 'in the image of God' than those who are physically 'unattractive'?

Beauty, we say, is in the eye of the beholder. Affected by the perspective of the celebrity culture, we find ourselves confused by pictures of perfection. In an age where we are bombarded with images of stereotypical physical ideals of the 'Barbie doll' sort, we diet and exercise to conform to supposed norms. Where does that leave disabled or disfigured people?

What is 'normal' and what is 'abnormal'? If physically able is 'normal', then is disabled 'abnormal'? This strange logic is offensive, to say the least. Are people who are physically or mentally disabled therefore not made in the image of God? Do they matter less than those who are so-called 'sound' of body and mind? History teaches us that when we reduce the status of some people to less than 'normal', we can find that we have given permission to treat them as less than human – as sub-human.

It goes without saying that disabled people are as prone to character flaws and bad behaviour as anyone else. As Christians, surely we recognize that we are all broken: that the image of God in us has been tainted or obscured, not by the way our mind or body works but by our failure to live as God intended. We have come to realize we need a saviour and have turned to Christ, who has dealt with our sin and is at work transforming us into his likeness – restoring us by degree to the perfection of God's image.

The Disability Wall

To say I'm made in the image of God is a statement about my status in the world: I am worthy of dignity, to be treated as somebody who represents something of God . . . We can pass one another by; we can say, 'That person isn't really my kind of person.' But God says you are made in God's image and so are they. You are invited to enrich your life by exploring what it means to be made in God's image, through that other person.   (Roy McCloughry)

In God's family we see people differently . . . We don't judge with the world's yardstick. We see each person as made in God's image, someone for whom Jesus Christ died.   (Jonathan Lamb)

There's no doubt about it. I am blind, that makes me different. The barriers can be reduced. But we all face a variety of challenges and barriers whether we say we are disabled or not.   (Mike Townsend)

The Church has so often got it so wrong in the past. Even the words we often use . . . are often fraught with difficulty because they are associated with negativity:

'*dis*-ability' . . . '*dis*-ease' . . . '*dis*-figured' . . . To love someone means to be able to look with integrity, with sincerity, into their eyes . . . to be able to say to them, 'It's good that you are you.'

(Bishop Michael Langrish)

I do not interpret my blindness as an affliction, but as a strange, dark and mysterious gift from God . . . it is a gift I would rather not have been given . . . Nevertheless, it is a kind of gift . . . it seems to me that it is blind people who are in the image of God rather than sighted people. Because of their dependence upon outward appearance and their confidence in being superior, it is often sighted people who are needy.   (Professor John Hull)

Real life: Alan Chantler

Alan first had cancer over 30 years ago.

That slowed me down . . . I spent a lot of time not able to rush about doing all the things that I thought were important and a lot of time thinking. I began to think that there was more to life than just ticking boxes, achieving things and showing other people what I'd achieved. I'd been given an opportunity to review my life and a strong signal that life was not what I could make all the time . . . I determined that I would try to do better.

Treatment was successful and Alan, a university academic, returned to work. Then, after some years, he began to experience back pain. A visit to the GP revealed nothing. Alan put the symptoms down to ageing and lack of exercise. On New Year's Day 2004 he went for a walk with friends and it was obvious to everyone that he was having difficulty walking – tripping over his own feet and struggling to get over stiles.

Alan was discovered to have a rare cancer of the spine. Surgery meant the removal of much of his spine and hence his mobility. These days he walks on two sticks or uses a wheelchair.

> When I woke up after the first operation on my back, a vision came to me of the stripes on our Lord's back when he had been scourged before crucifixion, and that gave me strength.

> Life deals out these things; you have to play the hand you've got. It's no use grizzling about what you wish might have happened.

> I can still sing. It gives me great delight to go to church every Sunday, put on my choir robes, stagger up the aisle into my place . . . I can't stand when others stand, I can't kneel when others kneel . . . but I can sing to the glory of God, and I thank him for that.

> Becoming disabled has actually made me a much better person. Every day is a bonus. My faith brings me the strength to stop and think about other people much more than I used to.

From an interview Alan gave to Torch Trust's Insight *radio programme.*

Real life: Denise Flynn

Constant stress over communication barriers and the effort to lip-read over many years made Denise Flynn ill.

> I was very tired physically and emotionally because of the stress of working out how to understand other people's language, year after year. One day I stopped using my voice and spoke only with sign language, wanting people to remember that I'm Deaf and that

I live in a silent world without sounds. Using sign language, my health improved and my daily headaches stopped.

Denise Flynn became Deaf as a baby. She was brought up in Buenos Aires, Argentina, where the oral school for Deaf children taught her Spanish.

Sign language was forbidden. However, at times I spoke it by hidden signing with my friends – for which I was sometimes punished by the teachers. Parents were trained not to allow children to use their hands. When I got married to David I began to have the freedom to use Bolivian Sign Language, later American Sign Language and then British Sign Language (BSL).

Denise received a good education and her parents were very supportive.

However, when I went to study medicine at university in Bolivia, after two years the lecturers began to tell me they were not happy with the idea of having a Deaf doctor. They had a perfectionist philosophy. So I qualified as a paramedic and in first aid but had to leave university. At that time there was nothing like the Disability Discrimination Act and no legal defence possible against my dismissal.

Although within the family everyone was supportive of me, outside the family I was so frustrated, particularly with lip-reading. Most of the time people thought their speech was clear for lip-reading and automatically treated me as a perfect lip-reader. They weren't patient enough to repeat things or make an effort to speak more clearly. They blamed me for the communication problems because it was easy for them to understand what I was saying. I wished many times that the hearing world were taught at school to learn how to speak to Deaf people.

God taught me a lot. Since becoming a Christian I've learned to accept myself as I am. There is no need for a Deaf person to pretend to be like a hearing person to try to integrate fully into the hearing world. Allowing a Deaf person to use sign language helps hearing people to understand visually the meaning of deafness, to see that we are different. We have a different language – using eyes rather than ears.

From the moment I believed God created me as a Deaf person in his image, I felt free from the negative outlook often heard from the non-disabled world. Common notions are, 'Deaf people are cursed by God', 'Deaf people can't do this or that', 'Deafness should be pitied and is an awful disease', 'Deafness needs to be fixed by the doctors' and so on.

Denise's search for a church was a long journey. After visiting 15 churches with her hearing husband she finally found a church community where, as she says, 'I was accepted as part of the family rather than attending a ceremony on Sundays.'

She attends a church in Tadworth, Surrey.

The leaders have a positive and flexible attitude to taking account of the issues for inclusion, such as providing interpreters. But it's more than interpreters. Deaf awareness training is provided and hearing people are encouraged to learn BSL and provide a support group which can approach Deaf people and make good relationships with them.

Has Denise been able to use her gifting in church?

Yes, I have given my testimony in the service and signed a poem at a Christmas service. I teach Deaf awareness and basic sign language. And I have been on a mission trip to Bolivia. Two hearing church members joined my mission trip to be involved in supporting me and serving the Bolivian people.

I feel valued at my church as they are supportive and always asking me questions such as, 'Are we improving our communication and including you?' Their humble attitude makes me feel loved. I feel like a human being rather than a dog tied to a lamp post at the church door.

Icebreaker question

Think of a disabled person you know – family member, friend, colleague. In turn, describe that person *without* making reference to any disability. When everyone has spoken, ask them to reveal the disability of the person described. Invite any disabled people present to talk about their lives, apart from their disability.

Questions for individual study or group discussion

Choose from this list:

- What does being made 'in the image of God' mean to you? And what do you think it means for society, with all its diversity?

- 'What we will be has not yet been revealed', writes the apostle John (1 John 3.2). How do you understand this? Does it change your view of human physicality?

- Models are ways of thinking about things. Read about the medical and social models of disability in the Author's Introduction (page 2). Debate the advantages and disadvantages of each. Where do you think concepts of community and relationship fit?

Taking it further

Choose from this list:

My story

What personal experience have you had of either temporary (for example, breaking an arm or leg) or long-term disability? This could be relatively trivial or life-changing. Discuss the impact on you, your family and friends.

Or

Ask people to think about something they are really good at, that they do well or that comes easily to them; and then ask them to think of something they can do relatively poorly or with difficulty. For example, perhaps they are good at speaking in public but feel awkward caring for small children. Invite them to describe that briefly in one or two sentences. After you have been around the group, ask everyone to imagine what it would be like always to be asked to do only the things they do badly, and never to have the opportunity to do what they do well. What would that feel like?

Or

Are there people who have become disabled during the time you have known them? Has your attitude – or the attitude of others – towards them changed? How? You might like to refer to Gordon Temple's and Alan Chantler's comments on the Disability Wall (pages 40 and 41).

In my locality

Name some groups in your community who experience prejudice or exclusion. Have available some copies of local and national newspapers for people to look through to give them ideas. Discuss the nature of the prejudice or exclusion. Is there anything that local church communities could or should do?

WWJD?

It's sometimes helpful to ask the question 'Would would Jesus do?' and this is a perspective we will turn to from time to time during the sessions.

Perhaps using a flipchart, brainstorm the different kinds of people with whom Jesus interacted positively or with affirmation – such as the woman at the well (John 4.1–26), people with leprosy (for example, Mark 1.40–45; Luke 17.11–19), tax collectors (such as Matthew 9.10–13). What does this show us about the way Jesus thought and felt? What does it reveal about the mission of Jesus?

Prayer

Give each person a small piece of card and a pen and ask everyone to write in a few words a group who might experience prejudice, such as 'drug addicts', 'immigrants', 'people with mental health conditions'. Collect the cards, shuffle, hand them around, one each, then pray in twos or threes for the named groups.

Or

Use this responsive prayer:

> Leader: Father, thank you for the diversity of the people you have created, each with something to show us about your character.

> All: We thank you, Lord, for all your people.

> Leader: Forgive us, Lord, for our lack of acceptance of each other's differences, for our cold-heartedness, for our judgemental spirit.

All: Forgive us, cleanse us and transform us, Lord.

Leader: We pray for more understanding of the peoples you have created, each with their own history and customs, their own culture, music and literature.

All: We thank you, Lord, for all your people.

Leader: Forgive us, Lord, for our intolerance of other nations, for our blindness to their distinctiveness, for our lack of interest in their ways.

All: Forgive us, cleanse us and transform us, Lord.

Leader: Thank you for the different people in our community, many coping with difficulties and pain, with hardship and weaknesses, with physical or mental challenges. All are unique and all individually known and loved by you.

All: We thank you, Lord, for all your people.

Leader: Forgive us, Lord, for barriers we have erected or maintained that have the effect of disabling some people, particularly physical and attitudinal barriers that stand in the way of full inclusion of all within our churches.

All: Forgive us, cleanse us and transform us, Lord.

Leader: Forgive us, Lord, for the times we have not reached out a hand of friendship or attempted to break down the barriers between us.

All: Forgive us, cleanse us and transform us, Lord. Amen.

2

Fearfully and wonderfully made

Exodus 4.10–12; Psalm 139.13–16; 2 Corinthians 4.7

Purpose: to explore the all-knowingness of God in the context of his plan for each person, with the acknowledgement that disability may be part of that; to consider that disability may be part of God's plan for our lives; to see strength in apparent weakness.

Prayer

- Thank God that we are each known by him in intimate detail, and that he loves us just as we are.
- Pray that each person attending the group will glimpse the wonder of acceptance by God for him or her as an individual.

Bible briefing

Moses said to the Lord, 'O my Lord, I have never been eloquent, neither in the past nor even now that you have spoken to your servant; but I am slow of speech and slow of tongue.' Then the Lord said to him, 'Who gives speech to mortals? Who makes them mute or deaf, seeing or blind? Is it not I, the Lord? (Exodus 4.10–12)

For it was you who formed my inward parts;
you knit me together in my mother's womb.
I praise you, for I am fearfully and wonderfully made.

Wonderful are your works;
that I know very well.
My frame was not hidden from you,
when I was being made in secret,
intricately woven in the depths of the earth.
Your eyes beheld my unformed substance.
In your book were written
all the days that were formed for me,
when none of them as yet existed.

(Psalm 139.13–16)

But we have this treasure in clay jars, so that it may be made clear that this extraordinary power belongs to God and does not come from us.

(2 Corinthians 4.7)

Bible briefing notes

God made us in his image – all of us – and he made us wonderful! Being 'made in the image' may not indicate a physical likeness, but the Psalmist sees in the miracle of our bodies evidence of the remarkable handiwork of God.

Some of the verses from Psalm 139 are put this way in *The Message* paraphrase: 'You know exactly how I was made, bit by bit . . . Like an open book, you watched me grow from conception to birth; all the stages of my life were spread out before you.'

Disability comes as no surprise to God. In his address to the reluctant Moses (Exodus 4.11), God takes responsibility for our faculties. This suggests planning, design, intent – not accident.

A thread running through the whole of Scripture is that of strength in apparent weakness. Tiny armies, like Gideon's, take on hugely superior forces and, in the strength God supplies, win convincingly. The shepherd boy David defeats the Philistine champion Goliath, over nine feet tall and clad in bronze armour. The young exile Daniel stands against the will of the egotistical Nebuchadnezzar and turns the king's heart to the true God. The apostle Paul, who himself seems to struggle with a disabling condition, hears from God: 'My grace is sufficient for you, for my power is made perfect in weakness' (2 Corinthians 12.9, NIV).

There's another perspective on this in the intriguing book of Job. When Job – bereaved, destitute and sick – complains about his plight, God turns the tables on him, letting fly a battery of questions: 'Do you know the ordinances of the heavens? Can you establish their rule on the earth? . . . Who has put wisdom in the inward parts, or given understanding to the mind?' (Job 38.33, 36). In doing so, God widens Job's perspective on life, the universe and everything.

Perhaps one way to define faith – Christian faith – is that it is *trusting God knows best, whatever* – that in whatever circumstances we find ourselves, we retain our confidence that God has not lost control, that God is not caught out, that God cares for us, that God has a plan for our lives.

Jesus didn't promise his followers a straightforward exist-ence. God's plan for our lives can include disability – for a period or for life. But whatever work God has for us, he will equip us to do it. Paul knew this (2 Corinthians 4.7). Not especially attractive, not particularly strong, earthen-ware pots were household utility items. Put under pressure, they would shatter. There are times when we all have to face our fragility. It's when we come to the end of our ability that God's ability is most evident in us.

Jesus went through the most disabling, humiliating ex-periences on the cross, but he did so with the definite understanding that it was part of Father God's plan. Even in the run-up to the crucifixion, he is blindfolded and taunted, entering into the vulnerability that a blind person might experience. Yet, in the apparent powerlessness of the cross, the greatest of victories was secured. We look to 'Jesus the pioneer and perfecter of our faith, who for the sake of the joy that was set before him endured the cross, disregarding its shame, and has taken his seat at the right hand of the throne of God' (Hebrews 12.2).

The Disability Wall

The glory of God is human beings fully alive.

(Irenaeus)

I'm from a charismatic background. The idea of abundant life for a charismatic is full of energy! Full of power! What does it look like if you can't stand up? Can't sing? Your arms don't work? If you see through the eyes of a guide dog? What does abundant life look like for people who live with disability?

(Malcolm Duncan)

We may think that God can only use the healthy and wealthy but the paradox of Christian experience is very different. God works through the weakness of the crucified Jesus and the disciples.

(Jonathan Lamb)

I was slightly brain-damaged at birth, and I want people like me to see that they shouldn't let a disability get in the way . . . I want to turn my disability into ability.   (Susan Boyle)

By taking human flesh and blood, God in Christ became disabled.   (Bob Brooke)

God comes to us as a disabled God, as a blind God, as a deaf God, and as a God whose power was shown ultimately in his weakness. (Nick Cook)

Weakness carries within it a secret power. The cry and the trust that flow from weakness can open up hearts. (Jean Vanier)

Disabled people are not incomplete examples of so called 'normal' humanity but are complete persons before God. Their impairments and disabilities are part of their human identity . . . God has called each one of us into being. None of us is a surprise or an accident or a mistake and certainly not an embarrassment to God. He has called us into being and each one of us has a vocation. (Bob Brooke)

What does it mean to be human? . . . Answering this question is likely to be the major moral and ethical issue facing us in the twenty-first century. Many of the already significant moral challenges have this as their root question: do we permit assisted suicide, experiments on embryos, saviour siblings, spare-part surgery, paid-for organs for transplant, remunerated surrogacy, not to mention euthanasia, human genetic manipulation, gender selection, human cloning – and doubtless many other procedures not yet imagined? (David Potter)

Real life: Kate Mancey

In her early teens, Kate developed a form of rheumatoid arthritis called Still's Disease. After a series of operations with complications, she went completely blind over a period of a few weeks, aged just 15. Withdrawn from formal schooling, Kate describes herself as 'isolated but self-sufficient'.

My peer group didn't know how to deal with me so I guess I felt I would help them out and disappear!

She pressed on with her long-held ambition to be a teacher, constantly having to break new ground to gain acceptance as a blind person.

For most things in life, as someone visually impaired, you have to be absolutely excellent. Mediocre won't do. It can be tiring to have to prove yourself in that way.

But Kate succeeded and loved teaching. She married Peter, and they had two daughters. Then her health further deteriorated. She had constant joint pain, and could hardly walk. She began to suffer from agoraphobia and that would alternate with claustrophobia. She became depressed, and hid away.

Inside I knew everything was falling apart. I felt a failure as a mum, a wife and a Christian.

This black period of her life went on for six or seven years before one evening someone prayed for her. She describes the experience as 'like being surrounded by a warm blanket ... all the joint pain went and the depression lifted. I felt like I'd got my life back ... it was a fresh start.'

Kate embarked on a new phase of her life, working alongside Peter as a speaker in churches, sharing her experiences, leading quiet days and running Alpha courses. She particularly loves to encourage other blind people and is a popular visiting speaker at Torch Trust's Holiday and Retreat Centre in Sussex, which offers specialist holidays to people with sight loss.

From an interview Kate gave to Torch Trust's Insight *radio programme.*

Real life: the Accept Project

Some simple ideas are the most brilliant. On the door of a shop front in a small Leicestershire town is the wording: 'Accept is an evolving Christian-based charity whose vision is to bring hope through friendship to people experiencing mental health problems.'

When a local day hospital closed, it meant the end of the 'smoke room' – a safe place where people with mental health problems could meet informally to share their problems and encourage one another. Aidan Lucas discussed with others how the smoke room ethos could be replicated in the community. This led to the Accept Project – informal groups of six to eight people meeting in pubs and cafes in the town, coordinated by a trained volunteer from one of the churches.

Aidan says,

> The groups are for people experiencing a wide range of enduring mental health problems such as schizophrenia, bipolar disorder, depression and anxiety – meeting not with a focus on their issues but on friendship and belonging. Often such people are very isolated. Each group decides its own activities. It might decide just to meet weekly for a chat or they might go for a meal, or go to the cinema.

> Real friendship is long-term, and that's the expectation within the groups. Success is measured by the friendships that have been built in the groups and how we've seen change in the people that belong to them.

> Many in the groups are now less fearful about going out in public. Some are confident enough to do their own shopping or even do some volunteering work.

> It's a great privilege to be involved in Accept. I've been through times myself of feeling isolated or depressed.

I know that God is always there, he loves us and accepts us and wants that to be demonstrated through one another, through care and friendship, just as Jesus did and continues to do. God's love is at the heart of Accept . . . reaching out to people just where they are.

K joined an Accept group from a background of abuse from childhood onwards, together with depression following the death of her mother.

I get panic attacks . . . Your heart races so fast and your legs go like jelly. You feel sick, like you're going to pass out. It makes you feel really rough.

The group has made a huge difference to my life. I've made a lot of friends which I haven't had before. People don't understand about mental illness. They just think, 'Pull yourself together.' But it's not that easy.

I've found real acceptance in the group. It's wonderful! We meet every Wednesday, we talk, have coffee. We've had one woman join us, P, and we're all going to her wedding and we're all looking forward to that.

Apart from the group, I don't really go out. I don't feel safe. I don't like crowds. I get frightened so easily because I had something really horrible happen to me. I'm frightened of people shouting at me because I've had a lot of abuse through my life. My ex-husband used to beat me up.

K says she loves Jesus and is happy to have found a supportive church. 'I could never do without God in my life.'

From interviews given to Torch Trust's Insight *radio programme.*

Questions for individual study or group discussion

Choose from this list:

- What examples can you think of from the Bible where apparent weakness actually triumphs over strength? Can you describe any examples from everyday life? What does this tell us about God's way of doing things?

- How comfortable are you with the idea of a God who 'makes' people deaf or blind (Exodus 4.11)? Reflect on the 'Real life' story of Paul and Edrie Mallard on page 76.

- Consider how you would begin to answer Malcolm Duncan's question from the Disability Wall (page 27): 'What does abundant life look like for people who live with disability?'

- Read about Kate Mancey on page 28. Thankfully Kate's 'black period', though lasting many years, came to an end. But many believing Christians live with depression and mental illness. Do you think there's a difference between the way we look at people with incapacitated bodies and people with incapacitated minds?

- David Potter's comment on the Disability Wall (page 28) takes us into some uncomfortable territory on the edges of disability debates: euthanasia and eugenics, for example. Has anything in these studies so far changed your views? Or confirmed your views?

Taking it further

Choose from this list:

In my locality

Work in pairs. Each of you should describe someone you know whom you consider to be beautiful. In what ways is the person beautiful?

Or

Read the 'Real life' report about the Accept Project on page 30. Does your church 'do' friendship well? How could it do it better?

WWJD?

As a group, describe the Hollywood portrayals you have seen of Jesus. Which was most attractive to you and why? Then read Isaiah 53.2b–5.

Or

Almost every disabled Christian has at some time been pressed to accept prayer by a well-intentioned Christian determined to pray for his or her healing, feeling that this would be 'what Jesus would do'. Often the disabled person would rather have prayer for the same issues as affect non-disabled people, maybe his or her finances or family situation. Discuss your views and experiences of this.

My story

Work in pairs, each answering the question, 'Who are you?' in one sentence. Discuss why you gave the answer you did. What was it based on? Your career? Your family relationships? Your relationship with Jesus? What do the different ways in which we define ourselves reveal about our self-image, our values or our faith? Share your conclusions with the whole group.

Or

With reference to the 'Real life' report about the Accept Project on page 30, discuss any experiences you've had of friendships that have been life-enhancing.

Prayer

Use this responsive prayer together, based on Psalm 139:

All: We bless you, Creator God, that you have made all things well.

Leader: For you formed my inward parts; you knit me together in my mother's womb.

All: Father, your children were all made to reflect your beauty and grace.

Leader: I praise you, for I am fearfully and wonderfully made; your works are wonderful, that I know very well.

All: Generous God, we rejoice in all you have made!

Leader: My frame was not hidden from you when I was being made in secret, intricately woven in the depths of the earth.

All: Give me joy in accepting myself as body, mind and soul that you delight in. Give me joy in accepting others as known and loved deeply by you.

Leader: Your eyes beheld my unformed substance; in your book were written all the days that were formed for me when none of them as yet existed.

All: Lord, your plans and purposes are mysterious to us, beyond our understanding, but we embrace them. Thank you for your extravagant love for us! Amen.

Or

DIY psalm

Using Bibles, work as individuals to create your personal versions of Psalm 139.13–16 in contemporary language ('You made me, right down to the smallest internal detail; starting with just two cells you fitted my tiny organs together in the right place when my mother was pregnant . . .) and share them aloud as a time of thanksgiving.

Or

Sing or say together the hymn 'O Love, that wilt not let me go' after reading about George Matheson in 'Hymn story' below.

Hymn story

George Matheson was one of eight children born in Glasgow in 1842. He always had impaired vision, wearing powerful glasses from childhood and later able to see only shadows. However, he was known for his optimism. He became a greatly respected preacher in Scotland and many of his congregation didn't realize he was blind.

His many writings include the famous hymn 'O Love, that wilt not let me go' which he wrote in a few minutes on the day of his sister's marriage in 1882, feeling that it had been dictated to him by an inner voice. He was asked to change only one word, substituting the word 'trace' for 'climb' in 'I climb the rainbow through the rain'. The more active verb is somehow significant when we remember he was a blind man – and perhaps rather more revealing of his life experience.

3
Standing up for justice

2 Samuel 4.4, 9.1–11; Mark 10.46–52

Purpose: to explore the idea of inclusion as a matter of justice, not charity; to look at self-worth, identity and dignity; to consider disabled people as contributors.

Prayer

- Pray that each person attending the group will feel engaged with the discussion and valued for his or her contribution.

Bible briefing

Note: Many people stumble over the name 'Mephibosheth'. To prevent this from inhibiting discussion, don't hesitate to refer to him as 'M' or 'Meffy'.

Saul's son Jonathan had a son who was crippled in his feet. He was five years old when the news about Saul and Jonathan came from Jezreel. His nurse picked him up and fled; and, in her haste to flee, it happened that he fell and became lame. His name was Mephibosheth . . .

David asked, 'Is there still anyone left of the house of Saul to whom I may show kindness for Jonathan's sake?' . . . Ziba said to the king, 'There remains a son of Jonathan; he is crippled in his feet.' . . . Mephibosheth . . . came to David, and fell on his face . . . 'I am your servant.' David said to him, 'Do not be afraid, for I will show you kindness for the sake of your father Jonathan; I will restore to you all the land of your grandfather Saul, and you yourself shall eat at my table always.' He did obeisance and said, 'What is your servant, that you should look upon a dead dog such as I am?'

Then the king summoned Saul's servant Ziba, and said to him, 'All that belonged to Saul and to all his house I have given to your master's grandson. You and your sons and your servants shall till the land for him, and shall bring in the produce, so that your master's grandson may have food to eat; but your master's grandson Mephibosheth shall always eat at my table'... Mephibosheth ate at David's table, like one of the king's sons.

(2 Samuel 4.4; 9.1–11)

As he and his disciples and a large crowd were leaving Jericho, Bartimaeus son of Timaeus, a blind beggar, was sitting by the roadside. When he heard that it was Jesus of Nazareth, he began to shout out and say, 'Jesus, Son of David, have mercy on me!' Many sternly ordered him to be quiet, but he cried out even more loudly, 'Son of David, have mercy on me!' Jesus stood still and said, 'Call him here.' And they called the blind man, saying to him, 'Take heart; get up, he is calling you.' So throwing off his cloak, he sprang up and came to Jesus. Then Jesus said to him, 'What do you want me to do for you?' The blind man said to him, 'My teacher, let me see again.' Jesus said to him, 'Go; your faith has made you well.' Immediately he regained his sight and followed him on the way.

(Mark 10.46–52)

Bible briefing notes

Mephibosheth or 'M' starts life in a privileged position as the grandchild of a reigning monarch. When news of the death of King Saul and his son Jonathan arrives, nurse and child make a hasty exit. In the ancient world, it was usual for all those associated with a former king or dynasty to be systematically eliminated. But in the flight to safety there's an accident and Mephibosheth becomes disabled.

Years later, we find him tucked away in rural obscurity. Lo Debar is in Gilead, the mountainous region on the east side of the Jordan. The name means 'without pasture' and hints at it being an 'out of the way' place. It seems that – as intended – Mephibosheth has been almost forgotten. He is at rock bottom. His self-description as 'a dead dog' has to be well down the self-worth scale.

Many disabled people find that in the minds of others their disability becomes their identity in a pejorative way: 'the blind woman' or 'that man in the wheelchair'. Nothing else about them seems to be of consequence – yet they may well lead full and active lives with family and work responsibilities, and they may have extraordinary stories, gifts and experience to share.

David's declared aim is to show kindness. But what he does goes a whole lot further than simple charity. Mephibosheth is restored, becoming once again part of the royal household, eating at the king's table – with his own property, responsibilities and income. As rock legend Bono famously said about giving to the needs of Africa, 'It's not charity, it's justice.' In fact, it's more than justice; it's grace.

Mephibosheth's disability appears not to make a jot of difference to David. We might reflect on Samuel's God-directed selection of David as future king from among his apparently more eligible older brothers. God's guidance to Samuel was: 'the LORD does not see as mortals see; they look on the outward appearance, but the LORD looks on the heart' (1 Samuel 16.7). Perhaps it was because David knew what it was to be overlooked and rejected that he behaves so well towards Mephibosheth. The 'dead dog' has his dignity restored, though his disability remains. It's worth considering that disabled people may regard their disability as an intrinsic component of their self-identity. While they may properly resent the imposition of disability as their defining characteristic, for them it can be an inseparable part of their personhood.

When Jesus encounters a blind man called Bartimaeus (Mark 10) he asks, 'What do you want me to do for you?' Bartimaeus does, in fact, want to receive his sight. But even Jesus – who probably knew the man's thoughts – does him the dignity of asking first.

And here's a general principle. Only recently has it become the norm for disabled people to be included in discussions about their medical and social care needs. Centuries before this modern phenomenon, Jesus sets a pattern for us to follow: always ask.

The Disability Wall

When I talk about disability being a strange gift, that doesn't mean it's all hunky dory. We're not all very happy to be who we are. There have been many days in my own life when I looked at God not as a God of love but as one who judged me prematurely by giving me something I didn't want . . . But God asks us to trust him and to believe he is good, and that what he has given us can be redeemed and used for his good purposes.   (Roy McCloughry)

Being at the receiving end of unwitting excluding behaviour on the part of so many people frequently leads to low self-esteem, lack of assertiveness and a minimal sense of value and significance among those with learning disabilities.

(John Naudé)

Even profoundly disabled people have gifts: among them is that of awakening our understanding of our own weakness and God's almighty power which includes us, even weak us, in his fellowship of power. (Mike Townsend)

Almost every time I meet somebody who has experienced the onset of disability they say something like, 'Since I've been in this wheelchair, people think I'm brain-dead.' Whatever has being in a wheelchair got to do with how your brain works and who you are as a person? (Gordon Temple)

Yes, I'm grateful for the drugs I take . . . but I don't want to be reduced to my biology. I want those who are around me . . . to actually look at my life as a whole. I don't want to feel like an object. I want to relate to others. (Jonathan Clark)

Even though I have rough moments in my wheelchair, for the most part I consider my paralysis a gift. Just as Jesus exchanged the meaning of the cross from a symbol of torture to one of hope and salvation, he gives me the grace to do the same with my chair. If a cross can become a blessing, so can a wheelchair. The wheelchair, in a sense, is behind me now. The despair is over. There are now other crosses to bear, other 'wheelchairs' in my life to be exchanged into gifts. (Joni Eareckson Tada)

What happens in the church is that people remember that you were this active person who ran up and down in a frock being a chorister and carrying the cross and running up and down the tower and ringing the bells and they can't understand why you are not doing it any more. So they wheel you in . . . because they know they are supposed to do that, but then they carry on and make conversations over the top of your head as though you don't exist.

(Alan Chantler)

Real life: Andrew Diaz-Russell

At the age of 20, Andrew was in a life-threatening medical crisis and his parents were told to prepare for his death.

Born prematurely with meningitis, Andrew developed hydrocephalus. A shunt was inserted in his brain to drain the fluid and as a child he became familiar with the operating theatre.

In his late teens he developed severe headaches and it was discovered that his catheter had calcified. During the operation to remove it, he picked up an infection which led to septicaemia of the brain. The inter-cranial pressure sent him into a coma for a week and a half. Doctors told Andrew's parents that his brain was 'the texture of toothpaste' and that if he survived he would be 'a vegetable'. When he woke he was totally blind and had many other medical problems – but his brain was fully functioning.

My survival . . . I don't know what else to call it but a miracle! And so is the fact that I no longer had hydrocephalus. Someone born with hydrocephalus dies with hydrocephalus. Also I've had meningitis twice – but I'm not deaf. And part of my brain was damaged . . . there is no medical explanation.

When Andrew was four years old, his father had explained the salvation possible because of Jesus' death on the cross, and he had prayed to be forgiven and follow Jesus. Through his near-death experience, Andrew re-committed his life to God.

Initially . . . I was desperate. I was trying hard to see something . . . maybe a shadow, maybe the sun . . . I had gone from perfect sight to zero . . . I kept asking God to give me back my sight. But angry with God? No! I know I am a sinner and deserve death, just like anyone else. But God in his grace has allowed me to be *only* blind and he gives me the grace to cope with it. I am thankful to the Lord because he is my strength and shield.

Andrew went on to finish his languages degree, and did an MA.

I started looking for work. Everyone who saw my white cane said, 'He can't do it!' So in the end, using my English, French and Spanish, I started working as a telephone interpreter. Nobody knows I am blind.

From an interview Andrew gave to Torch Trust's Insight *radio programme.*

Real life: Sarah Redgrove

Sarah has learning disabilities. But her problems weren't diagnosed until she was an adult – which meant a troubled childhood.

I wasn't quite like other children. I struggled all the way through school, knowing I couldn't get anywhere. Every time I tried to learn I used to get frustrated and go absolutely berserk. I went to a boarding school and used to get very upset.

There were some dark times for Sarah. Sometimes she felt life wasn't worth living. But things began to change when she got a diagnosis of learning disabilities and was put in touch with a Prospects group in another town, a group for people just like her. She began to feel more positive and purposeful.

I always knew I was loved by something, but I didn't know what . . . I wanted to end my life, but something was stopping me and I didn't know what that was. Now I know it was Jesus! Absolutely brilliant!

At Prospects, they helped me to learn about Jesus, how he died for us, and about forgiving everybody.

These days Sarah is living in warden-controlled accommodation, attends college two days a week, and helps out with the horses at the family's stables business.

Now I'm learning maths and English at Lincoln College and I'm really pleased about that. It's still a struggle. But I have a lot of support.

Sarah has a full social life. She became the founding member of a local Prospects group and finds her diary is full with outings, hobbies and Bible studies with her friends.

I was praying for 13 years that we'd get a group in Lincoln. We started off at the beginning with just ten of us and we thought, 'Oh, it's not going to work!' But now we've got just over 30 . . . building with God, knowing who Jesus is and giving their lives to him, it's marvellous to see that!

More than that, Sarah has become an advocate, often speaking in public about the needs of the 1.5 million people in the UK with learning disabilities. A particular highlight was meeting David Cameron and speaking at the House of Commons as part of an initiative to recruit people of influence as ambassadors for Prospects.

From an interview Sarah gave to Torch Trust's Insight *radio programme.*

Questions for individual study or group discussion

Choose from this list:

- Where does a sense of self-worth come from? Is it from education and qualifications, from job or professional status, from good looks, from friends and families, from the approval of others? How secure are these as a basis for our self-esteem?

- Discuss the impact of disability on self-image. Look at Mephibosheth's description of himself as 'a dead dog' in the 2 Samuel passage. Use the sometimes contradictory comments on the Disability Wall (page 39–41) to inform your discussion.

- Would Stephen Hawking – a university physicist – have become such a household name if he didn't have motor neurone disease? Think about others in the public arena associated with disability, such as David Blunkett or Stevie Wonder. How do you think their disability has affected their careers? Take account in your discussion of Kate Mancey's comment on mediocrity on page 29.

- King David took responsibility for restoring Mephibosheth's fortunes. Who takes responsibility for championing disabled people in our society, our community, our church? Whose responsibility should it be? Is this purely a local question or a matter of the bigger picture of justice and grace? Think about Bono's comment referred to in the Bible briefing notes: 'It's not charity, it's justice' (page 38), which is followed by Gordon Temple saying: 'In fact, it's more than justice; it's grace.' How can we express both justice and grace in our relationships with disabled people?

• What difference does it make when we look at the inclusion of disabled people as a matter of justice instead of a matter of charity? Look at the 'Real life' report on Andrew Diaz-Russell on page 41. Is it right that he has to find a way of working that hides his blindness from his clients?

Taking it further

Choose from this list:

In my locality

Describe initiatives in your community which enable marginalized people to be 'restored' from situations in which they have felt second-best or overlooked.

WWJD?

Recall some of the encounters that Jesus had with disabled people. Yes, he healed many whose stories are told in the Gospels, but in what other ways did he encourage positive feelings of self-worth?

Or

Look at Jesus in the healing of blind Bartimaeus (Mark 10) and discuss what this shows about his attitude to people with disability.

My story

Think about negative experiences in your life that have robbed you of self-esteem. In pairs, share one of your stories briefly with each other. Has this experience left scars? Has this issue been resolved for you or is it ongoing? Pray thoughtfully for each other.

Junk or jewels?

Scatter a pile of 'junk' in the corner of the room or space you are meeting in. You could use crushed drinks cans, empty food cans, glass jars and bottles, maybe some old CDs. While everyone watches, take a dustpan and brush and sweep everything into a pile. As you do so, talk about how some people feel like 'rubbish' because they are disabled or damaged in some way; or have someone else read out comments from the Disability Wall. Place a tray of sand in front of the pile. Invite people to come forward and light a candle, placing it in the sand as they name groups or individuals in the community who might feel like 'rubbish'. Dim the main lights. Point out how the light of prayer on the junk items gives them beauty; they shine and glimmer in the candlelight. Invite people to pray aloud for broken individuals; and for those who feel discarded because of their disability. You might like to revisit the story of Alan Chantler (page 16).

Prayer

Read the 'Real life' report on page 41. Andrew is a talented interpreter. He works internationally, using the telephone and computer connections. Pray for disabled people who find it difficult to find employment. Sometimes this is because their education has been impacted by their disabilities. Sometimes it's because of prejudice in the workplace.

4

Experiencing God in togetherness

Genesis 2.18–22; Psalm 68.5, 6; John 17.20–23

Purpose: to explore God-given models of community; to consider the challenge of isolation and loneliness as a particular issue for disabled people.

Prayer

- Pray that each person attending the group will understand more about the rich diversity of what it means to be in community – together with one another and with God.

- Ask God for the gift of exceptional love for fellow Christians.

Bible briefing

Then the LORD God said, 'It is not good that the man should be alone; I will make him a helper as his partner.' So out of the ground the LORD God formed every animal of the field and every bird of the air, and brought them to the man to see what he would call them; and whatever the man called each living creature, that was its name . . . but for the man there was not found a helper as his partner. So the LORD God caused a deep sleep to fall upon the man . . . he took one of his ribs and closed up its place with flesh. And the rib that the LORD God had taken from the man he made into a woman and brought her to the man. (Genesis 2.18–22)

Father of orphans and protector of widows
is God in his holy habitation.
God gives the desolate a home to live in.

(Psalm 68.5, 6)

'I ask not only on behalf of these, but also on behalf
of those who will believe in me through their word,
that they may all be one. As you, Father, are in me and
I am in you, may they also be in us, so that the world
may believe that you have sent me. The glory that you
have given me I have given them, so that they may be
one, as we are one, I in them and you in me, that they
may become completely one, so that the world may
know that you have sent me and have loved them
even as you have loved me.'   (John 17.20–23)

Bible briefing notes

From Genesis 1 we learned that God created the universe
and all that is in it – and that he created us all in his
image. God's own reflection on his creation is that it is
'good', 'very good'. Life in this environment is idyllic. That
is, until Genesis 3, when the proto-couple assert their
independence and break the only constraint placed upon
them by their Creator – not to eat from the tree of the
knowledge of good and evil. This we call the Fall and,
from here on, the Bible narrative takes on a darker tone
as the one sin becomes many, while God works tirelessly
to restore the perfection of his creation.

Quite recently someone asked me something which at
first I took to be a trick question: 'What was *not* good
before the Fall?' Doubtless some of you will 'get it' in a
moment, but others, like me, will struggle. In Genesis 2
God looks at the first man and observes, 'It is not good
that the man should be alone.' It's a passage often read
at weddings; the text goes on to explain the creation of

woman and the relationship between man and woman. But I think it also reveals a principle of wider application.

'Let *us* make humankind in *our* image' says God (Genesis 1.26). Notice the plurals. Though there is but one true God, Scripture introduces us to God as the Trinity: Father, Son and Holy Spirit. God is community – one God in three persons. There is a perfect and unending relationship between them; and in the creation of humanity they act collectively. It is therefore not a surprise that God recognizes that something vital is missing when Adam stands alone.

Though we may seek solitude from time to time, we are not designed for solitary existence. As clergyman and poet John Donne famously wrote, 'No man is an Island, entire of itself; every man is a piece of the Continent, a part of the main.'

Loneliness is an unattractive, undesirable condition. It is unnatural for us to be so dislocated from our community that we become lonely. It's disturbing that so many disabled people experience great loneliness and social isolation. According to 2009 NHS statistics, more than one million disabled people live alone, about one in ten compared to one in 12 of the general population. As many as 45 per cent of blind people may live alone; and the Alzheimer's Society estimates that one in three of people with dementia live alone.

In the formative years of the Church, pioneers evidently took care of widows among their congregations (Acts 6.1ff.). Recent challenges from Britain's politicians to foster 'the big society' are nothing new! Appointments were made to fulfil this responsibility in a way that was adequate to the need and with godly wisdom. Church is the community of God's people on earth and 'family' is a good word to capture the nature of the relationships that should characterize church life.

For some disabled people the word 'community' conjures up unhelpful connotations of institutional living that was the norm in years gone by; having said that, it's important not to lose 'community' – properly understood – as an essential ingredient of all our lives.

So to John 17. It's a remarkable moment, just hours before Jesus' arrest and crucifixion. This is the longest recorded prayer of Jesus that we have. He prays first for himself and then for those who have travelled with him for three years. But then he widens the circle to include all who come to believe in him through the testimony of those eye-witness disciples. And that includes us. Jesus was praying for you and me!

Three times he prays that we may be 'one'. Did he already know how challenging the issue of Christian unity was going to be? Why is this so important to Jesus?

First, it reflects God's intent in creation. Jesus presents the quality of relationship that exists within the Trinity as the benchmark for relationships among his followers. This is an extraordinary concept. He gives us a model of oneness which he longs for us to experience: 'that they be one, as we are one'.

But there's another reason. He sees it as fundamentally important to the success of our mission to the world. The implication is that we can't expect anyone to be interested in the gospel of Christ if there isn't clear evidence of exceptional fellowship among those claiming to be his followers. Could it be that the way that disabled people are received and included within church communities might be part of that evidence?

Paul writes to Christians in Rome: 'Let love be genuine . . . love one another with mutual affection; outdo one another in showing honour' (Romans 12.9, 10).

The Disability Wall

According to RNIB, 100 people a day in Britain are told that they are losing their sight. When given that diagnosis, only one in five has anyone with them who could effectively support them in understanding what's happening, where they go from here and how they cope with the whole experience. Only one in 12 is ever offered any form of counselling. Yet the pattern of loss and grief of people experiencing the onset of disability is understood to be very similar to the experience of bereavement: denial, anger, guilt, depression and acceptance. It's a journey that's too often travelled alone. (Gordon Temple)

To be lonely is to feel unwanted and unloved, and therefore unlovable. Loneliness is a taste of death. No wonder some people who are desperately lonely lose themselves in mental illness or violence to forget the inner pain. (Jean Vanier)

... all persons with and without disabilities are ... called to an inclusive community in which they are empowered to use their gifts. This inclusive community of all the people of God is holy in Christ irrespective of the physical state of their bodies and level of psychological functioning.
(From the statement of faith by the
Ecumenical Disability Advocates Network
of the World Council of Churches, EDAN)

Interdependence is at the heart of Christianity.
(Mike Townsend)

Losing your world

Professor John Hull likens becoming blind to becoming a citizen of a different world.

> If someone is born into a disabled condition, the world generated by that state is formed from the earliest days. One is, so to speak, born a citizen of that world. On the other hand, if one becomes disabled at a later stage, whether during childhood or in adult life, one experiences the shock of losing one's world. The tendency is for resistance, and then for a terrible sense of loss, and then the disabled body shrinks back into itself. One becomes extremely conscious of having an impaired body, whether it is merely a broken arm or leg, or losing the power of speech following a stroke, or loss of mobility after an accident. It is then true that whereas most people live in the world, disabled people live in their bodies . . . The normal world regards the disabled person as banished, excluded, deprived, as it were, of citizenship rights, and as therefore to be pitied and helped.
>
> As the recently disabled person recovers from the shock of the fractured and now lost world, a new world gradually begins to dawn . . . The body builds up its new world, relating to it with new powers and functions for different parts of the body. In the case of the blind person, the hands are no longer mainly used to do things, but now to know things and finally to appreciate beauty.
>
> As the new world is gradually built up, put into place with innumerable fits and starts, the disabled person is no longer confined to the broken body, but begins again to inhabit a world. No longer merely an exile, he or she applies for and is granted citizenship of a new place. The body is again integrated within

its world and the former world remains as a dream, an occasional flash of regret, a pang, perhaps, only to be overtaken by the intrinsic meaning of the new world within which one must not only exist but must live.

This is taken from a longer piece of writing called 'A spirituality of disability: the Christian heritage as both problem and potential' which is well worth reading and is available online at ‹www.johnmhull.biz/A%20Spirituality%20of%20 Disability1.htm›.

Real life: Tracy Williamson

Tracy is profoundly deaf and has sight loss – but that doesn't prevent her from having a deep personal spirituality and a significant writing and speaking ministry. It may seem ironic, but what Tracy's ministry centres on is 'listening to God'. She's had five books published on this subject and regularly runs workshops.

Tracy first discovered the joys of writing in her late teens.

I love seeing things that are beautiful and meaningful and exploring those in words.

Then later Tracy began a practice she calls 'prayer journalling'. She first used it on retreat. She recorded what she was feeling, the ways God was touching her, sometimes writing down deep struggles from her past. She began to listen to what God might be saying in response, so it became a bit like a conversation on paper.

We can all hear God if we put our lives in his hands, but many people believe that they can't hear him. God is a Father who loves to hear from his children, so when we share our hearts with him he wants to speak back to us. He wants to give wisdom, understanding and new perspectives. When I listen to God, then I know that he can turn my life around, he can give revelation about a particular area of need.

In her workshops, Tracy teaches people to 'prayer journal'. Often people who come have low self-esteem or a sense of failure, or see themselves as disappointments. Through prayer journalling and listening to God, many experience life-changing healing or fresh insights.

From an interview Tracy gave to Torch Trust's Insight *radio programme.*

Real life: Timothy Bamber

Timothy is autistic and partially sighted. Several times he has visited the Iona ecumenical Christian community off the west coast of Scotland, a place where he feels especially accepted. His father David is usually his guide. A typical week on Iona includes services morning and evening in the ancient abbey, workshops and a seven-mile pilgrimage around the island, including a stop at the landing place of Saint Columba, who brought Christianity to the area.

David: Iona is all about being welcomed and included. It's always emphasized that it's not a retreat; it's a place where you go to join in, to be active. People who come do all the chores, except the cooking. If I think about the team who run the holiday weeks, and their attitude, the word 'inclusive' comes to mind.

Timothy: I try to take part in most things, but it's a challenge. But that's what makes it so special.

David and Timothy last visited Iona at Christmastime.

David: Often when we visit, Timothy is the only
disabled person, but that Christmas
there were several. On the last day we all
participated in a service. Timothy wanted
to take part and he wrote and read a
prayer. He wrote it on his little electronic
Braille machine. That was the first time
in public he successfully used it on the
lectern. I really don't know anywhere
else where he has participated in a service
as much.

Timothy: It was a great experience to take part – a
moment to take away.

David: Gradually, as the week goes on, you get
closer and closer together in this community
of people. By the end, you are really part
of it . . . you've had this really beautiful
build-up of friendship, inclusiveness and
spirituality.

Timothy's favourite Iona song is 'Goodness is stronger
than evil', the words originally by Desmond Tutu, adapted
and put to music by John Bell of the Iona Community:

Goodness is stronger than evil;
Love is stronger than hate;
Light is stronger than darkness;
Life is stronger than death.
Victory is ours, victory is ours, through him
who loved us.

From interviews David and Timothy gave to Torch Trust's
Insight *radio programme.*

Questions for individual study or group discussion

Choose from this list:

- Psalm 68 describes God as the 'father of orphans and protector of widows' and says that he 'gives the desolate a home'. How do we square this with the obvious signs of deep loneliness in our society? How can we be engaged as God's agents in responding to loneliness in our communities?

- What are the essential characteristics of community? Thinking of your own life, in which communities do you participate? How easy is it for disabled people to play a full part in those communities? What expressions of community might be most inclusive of disabled people? What about, for example, online communities?

- Some disabled people have lived with disability all their lives; it is part of their identity. Some experience the onset of disability through accident, illness, genetic predisposition or ageing. With reference to the quote from Gordon Temple on the Disability Wall (page 51), how might your church respond to those on that journey?

- Read John Hull's moving description of the transition to blindness as the transfer of citizenship to a new world (page 52). How is this like and unlike moving from the world of the unbeliever to the believer?

Taking it further

Choose from this list:

My story

In pairs, share any experiences of loneliness you've experienced or are experiencing. Can you describe any factors which contributed/are contributing to your aloneness? Pray for each other.

Or

How can the experience of bereavement be compared to the loss of sight or hearing or mobility? Encourage people in the group with relevant experiences to share their thoughts.

Inclusive Communion

Communion is the part of church worship that best expresses the intentional unity among Christians. Write a short description of a variety of disabilities (e.g. wheelchair user, blind, Deaf, Parkinson's, learning disability, autism, etc.) on enough slips of paper to include everyone in the group. Hand out the slips randomly. Ask the group to discuss how Communion might be celebrated in a manner that includes them all, with each person approaching it from the point of view of their adopted disability.

WWJD?

Do you think loneliness or isolation were experiences that Jesus knew as a man? When, or in what circumstances? Share your ideas.

In my locality

Read about how Timothy Bamber (page 54) feels loved and accepted by the Iona Community. What about those who don't have anywhere where they feel included? Where do you feel most accepted? Describe your experiences and pray for each other.

Or

Read about Tracy Williamson (page 53). Think about the ministries for the encouragement and blessing of the local church that might be dormant in disabled people you know. Discuss how you might go about discovering and releasing them.

Worship with song

Read aloud the words of Timothy Bamber's favourite Iona song, 'Goodness is stronger than evil' from page 55. If you'd like to get hold of it to play during the session it's on the Iona CD *Love and Anger*, available from ‹www.ionabooks.com›.

Prayer

Don't forget that carers, too, can feel lonely and long for a safe place to be and to belong. Pray for any known to the group who are full-time carers for a disabled family member, that God will give them patience, strength and joy. And pray for professional carers, that God's love will inform all they do.

Or

Read Nick Cook's comment on the Disability Wall (page 28). Think about God making himself vulnerable (as he did in Jesus) to identify with your circumstances. Go around the group, offering single-sentence prayers of thanks for what that means to you.

5

Entering the Gate called Beautiful

Acts 3.1–10, 16; Luke 5.17–26; John 9.1–3

Purpose: to identify barriers to worship that might keep disabled people distanced from Jesus; to explore ideas of stigma, inclusion, forgiveness, healing and wholeness.

Prayer

- Pray that each person attending the group will experience the healing love of Jesus in his or her life.
- Ask God for eyes to see beyond the physical appearance of things.

Bible briefing

One day Peter and John were going up to the temple at the hour of prayer, at three o'clock in the afternoon. And a man lame from birth was being carried in. People would lay him daily at the gate of the temple called the Beautiful Gate so that he could ask for alms from those entering the temple. When he saw Peter and John about to go into the temple, he asked them for alms. Peter looked intently at him, as did John, and said, 'Look at us.' And he fixed his attention on them, expecting to receive something from them. But Peter said, 'I have no silver or gold, but what I have I give you; in the name of Jesus Christ of Nazareth, stand up and walk.' And he took him by the right hand and raised him up; and immediately his feet and ankles were made strong. Jumping up, he stood and began to walk, and he entered the temple with them, walking and leaping and praising God. All the people saw him walking and praising God, and they recognized him as the one who used to sit and ask for alms at the Beautiful Gate of the temple; and they were filled with wonder and amazement at what had happened to him. (Acts 3.1–10)

One day, while he was teaching, Pharisees and teachers of the law were sitting nearby . . . the power of the Lord was with him to heal. Just then some men came, carrying a paralysed man on a bed. They were trying to bring him in and lay him before Jesus; but finding no way to bring him in because of the crowd, they went up on the roof and let him down with his bed through the tiles into the middle of the crowd in front of Jesus. When he saw their faith, he said, 'Friend, your sins are forgiven you.' Then the scribes and the Pharisees began to question, 'Who is this who is speaking blasphemies? Who can forgive sins but God alone?' When Jesus perceived their questionings, he answered them, 'Why do you raise such questions in your hearts? Which is easier, to say, "Your sins are forgiven you", or to say, "Stand up and walk"? But so that you may know that the Son of Man has authority on earth to forgive sins' – he said to the one who was paralysed – 'I say to you, stand up and take your bed and go to your home.' Immediately he stood up before them, took what he had been lying on, and went to his home, glorifying God. Amazement seized all of them, and they glorified God and were filled with awe, saying, 'We have seen strange things today.' (Luke 5.17–26)

As he walked along, he saw a man blind from birth. His disciples asked him, 'Rabbi, who sinned, this

man or his parents, that he was born blind?' Jesus
answered, 'Neither this man nor his parents sinned;
he was born blind so that God's works might be
revealed in him.'   (John 9.1–3)

Bible briefing notes

When a paralysed man is carried to Jesus (Luke 5) by his
four friends, they have to improvise their own accessibility
arrangements – lowering him through the roof of the house
where Jesus is addressing a group of religious types. What
impeded a more conventional entrance? A lack of level
access? Or maybe too narrow a doorway? Not a bit of it!
The problem was the people blocking the way – a problem
often experienced by today's wheelchair users. It's obvious
to the self-important religious leaders that it's they who
should be closest to Jesus.

The paralysed man shares the stigma of the blind man we
meet in John 9. The man's presenting need is his paralysis.
But before he attends to that, Jesus first addresses the
man's sin by pronouncing forgiveness. To us this may seem
a bit hard on the paralysed man; after all, what opportunity
did he have for a life of sin? Rather less than the others
in the room, I imagine! What Jesus is doing is addressing
the universal assumption of his self-righteous onlookers
that the man is disabled as a punishment for sin. Jesus'
pronouncement of forgiveness relieves the man of this
stigma before he puts him on his feet. We might say he
is made whole before he is healed. The visible act of the
man's healing validates the invisible act of forgiveness.

The connection between disability and sin is still made
by people in many parts of the world. Now, of course,
sin *can* lead to disability. For example, a person might be
disabled by a road traffic accident that he or she caused
by driving dangerously. But it's not necessarily the case.

When the disciples pose a question to Jesus that today we find outrageous (John 9.2), his response is to break the assumed link. He offers an explanation for the man's blindness that we would surely want to be true of us in our own circumstances: 'he was born blind so that God's works might be revealed in him'.

The encounter between Peter, John and the disabled man (Acts 3) happens at three in the afternoon, a time of prayer when there's a peak in traffic into the Temple courts. He has been carried there to a pinch-point in the flow of people – presumably by friends like those who lowered the paralysed man through the roof. Everyone going into the Temple courts would pass him. Unable to work or grow food, he's there every day, begging for small change. Everyone knows him.

The setting for this encounter is highly significant. Herod's Temple was a huge place. The Gate called Beautiful was the entrance into the inner Temple courts. While anyone could come within the outer wall, there were strict rules about who could pass the Beautiful Gate. There was the Court of Women into which only those who were Jews, both men and women, could pass. But only Israelite men could progress further into the Court of Israel. Beyond this were courts restricted to the priesthood. Finally, at the heart of the Temple was an ancient skyscraper of a building. Standing 15 storeys tall, it was separated into two chambers divided by an enormous curtain: the Holy Place and the Holy of Holies. The latter was understood to be God's dwelling place on earth and could be entered but once a year by just one person, the serving High Priest.

In effect, to progress through the Temple courts was to pass a sequence of 'no entry' signs. It was an exclusion system that modelled in masonry the Jewish understanding of holiness and 'cleanness'.

It was not just because of the density of traffic in and out of the inner Temple courts that the disabled man was begging at the Beautiful Gate. He would not have been allowed to go further. All disabled and disfigured people were excluded from the Temple courts beyond the Beautiful Gate. Once he has been healed, the disabled man is free to accompany Peter and John into the Temple courts, exuberant in his worship. This is a story of access!

When Jesus enters the Temple after his triumphal entry into Jerusalem he doesn't like what he sees. Not only is the system of money changing and dove selling corrupt, but it's also regulating access to the Temple – and to forgiveness.

In the confusion that follows Jesus' direct action against the money changers and dove sellers, 'the blind and the lame' came to Jesus in the Temple courts where they were not allowed (Matthew 21.12–14). The people who had been kept out were now inside – and without being healed first. Jesus had thrown the barriers at the Gate called Beautiful wide open. And when he died on the cross a few days later, the innermost barrier – the great curtain of the Holy of Holies – was mysteriously and irreparably torn top to bottom. 'It is finished' is the unmistakable message.

The Disability Wall

If I regarded my life from the point of view of the pessimist, I should be undone. I should seek in vain for the light that does not visit my eyes and the music that does not ring in my ears. I should beg night and day and never be satisfied. I should sit apart in awful solitude, a prey to fear and despair. But since I consider it a duty to myself and to others to be happy, I escape a misery worse than any physical deprivation. (Helen Keller)

Disability is not a brave struggle or 'courage in the face of adversity'. Disability is an art. It's an ingenious way to live. (Neil Marcus)

Not only do physically disabled people have experiences which are not available to the able-bodied, they are in a better position to transcend cultural mythologies about the body, because they cannot do things the able-bodied feel they must do in order to be happy, 'normal' and sane . . . If disabled people were truly heard, an explosion of knowledge of the human body and psyche would take place.

(Susan Wendell)

What does it mean to be whole? For me, it's knowing my true worth and identity in Christ. My disability is one part of who I am. My desire is to follow Christ. It's not about walking. It's about becoming more and more like him. (John Naudé)

It is important, I think, to distinguish between curing and healing. Curing means the removal of the condition and all its symptoms; healing implies being restored to wholeness, growing in spiritual wellbeing so that someone can be healed while still living with the symptoms of a particular illness or condition. For some people healing might take place as they begin to move on from the sense of loss and grief they feel to an acceptance of the situation they find themselves in – moving from asking the question 'Why?' to asking, 'What does God want me to do with my life? How is he going to work through me with all the limitations that I have?' All of us, disabled or non-disabled, need healing. (Bob Brooke)

Real life: Miles Hilton-Barber

Miles grew up in Zimbabwe, where his father was director of civil aviation. Fascinated by aeroplanes, Miles's desire was to be a pilot and he went along to join the Rhodesian Air Force after finishing school. And that's when a routine medical check revealed that he was going blind with a hereditary disease called retinosa pigmentosa.

> It was a big shock – and the first thing I did was to ignore it. I was like an ostrich with my head stuck in the sand. As my eyesight deteriorated, I lost my confidence, my dignity and my independence. I didn't want anything to do with blindness, so my horizons diminished.

> I had become a Christian a couple of years before and I figured that sooner or later God would heal me. When he didn't heal me, I thought it was because of my lack of faith. But finally the Lord got through to me. He made me understand that he could reveal more of his grace, goodness and love to the world through me by giving me the ability to live a totally happy and productive life as a blind man. And that's certainly what's happened.

But what about Miles's ambition to become a pilot? When Miles reached the age of 50, his elder brother – now also totally blind through the same hereditary condition – built a 32-foot yacht in his back garden and announced that he was going to sail solo from South Africa to Australia. With speech output on his navigation instruments, Geoffrey sailed 53 days alone across the most dangerous ocean in the world.

> What my brother did made me realize that my problem was not my blindness but my attitude to my blindness. I needed to focus on my dreams – not on my

circumstances. So I learned to fly, and flew from London to Sydney in a microlight.

Since then, Miles has flown other aircraft and set other flying records. 'And I hold the record for being the first blind pilot to vomit at supersonic speeds!'

Miles says that he achieved all this and many other amazing physical achievements despite being a child who lacked self-confidence.

But the most radical part of the transformation was learning through the Scriptures that happiness is not based on circumstances but on how you respond to them.

From an interview Miles gave to Torch Trust's Insight *radio programme.*

Real life: Clemmie Elliott

Rebecca Elliott had what she describes as a 'perfect pregnancy' – followed by a terrible labour, resulting in an emergency Caesarian. Clemmie was born profoundly physically and mentally disabled with cerebral palsy. Examining a scan when she was five months old, the neurologist said the baby's brain damage was the second-worst case he'd seen in 25 years.

It was a slap in the face. Our dreams were shattered. But you feel closest to God in the midst of a tragedy.

She will never walk or talk, let alone ride a bike or all the rest of it. But Clemmie is just wonderful! She smiles most of the time, she's very content, she doesn't get jealous or annoyed, doesn't complain, doesn't want for things she doesn't have. She's just beautiful and perfect and we love her to bits.

So much of what you hear in the media about profoundly disabled children is negative and our experience has been a positive one. Obviously, there has been heartache. Obviously, there have been difficulties. But Clemmie has brought an enormous amount of pleasure into our lives – and to everyone who meets her. She's just delightful.

In contrast to the society we live in, which is all about achievement, Clemmie's life is different. She's not going to *do* anything – she just *is*. And that teaches us something about the value of life for life's sake.

The wonderful and close interaction between Clemmie and her younger brother Toby has prompted Rebecca to launch into a new career. After eight years in book illustration she has now become a successful children's writer, which she describes as a 'dream job'. Her picture books have been acclaimed for their positive view of disability.

Disabled children should be able to see themselves represented more in the books that are written for them.

From an interview Rebecca gave to Torch Trust's Insight *radio programme.*

Questions for individual study or group discussion

Choose from this list:

- Think of the instances of exclusion experienced by sick, disfigured or disabled people in the New Testament accounts (including those mentioned in the Bible briefing on page 59). How might the experience of disabled people of today compare?

- Think about the stigmatizing of disabled people that Jesus addresses head-on in John 9. 'Who sinned?' he is asked. His answer is along the lines of 'Wrong question!' His explanation about the works of God being displayed is much more interesting. How do you respond?

- Bob Brooke's comment on the Disability Wall (page 64) draws our attention to the distinction between 'healing' and 'curing'. Do you agree with the distinction he draws? Can a person be made 'whole' without physical healing? How does this affect our understanding of the ministry of the Church?

- Some of our churches have been constructed to mimic artists' impressions of the Temple in Jerusalem. Think about your church, its architecture and furnishings. What are the barriers to access – both physical and symbolic? How could they be reduced, removed or improved?

Taking it further

Choose from this list:

Drama at the Beautiful Gate

Choose three people to have speaking parts in 'Drama at the Beautiful Gate', using the script below. The rest of the group can take parts they choose for themselves. One could be John; the rest could be passers-by, beggars or Temple officials. Their task is to observe and to react to what happens.

The storyteller:	It's the hour for prayer, three o'clock in the afternoon. In the heat and dust at the foot of the Beautiful Gate lies a disabled man well known to everyone who passes by. He cannot walk. Generally they ignore him. He is there every day, asking for

handouts from those going up to the Temple. He's never been inside, not since he has been disabled. It wouldn't be right; it would be inappropriate and it's against the Temple regulations.

Man: Have mercy on me! Just a few small coins! Anything! Almighty God will show favour to you if you help keep me alive.

The storyteller: Then the lame man sees Peter and John, followers of Jesus, approaching the gate. He holds out his hands, expecting to get something from them. They stop and look him in the eyes.

Peter: We have no money. Nothing at all! Yet we will gladly give you what we have. In the name of Jesus Christ of Nazareth, I command you to get up and walk!

The storyteller: Peter reaches out a hand and helps him up. Amazed, the lame man feels strength and vitality flooding into his legs, feet and ankles. He gets to his feet, his eyes widening. He walks into the Temple – yes, right into the Temple! – with the two disciples, where he begins to jump up and down.

Man: I can walk! Look, everyone! I can walk! Thanks be to God! God has had mercy on me. I am healed! Now I can enter the Beautiful Gate and worship the Lord with everyone else!

The storyteller: There is uproar! Everyone is completely surprised by what is happening.

Peter: Don't look so amazed! And don't think for one minute that it's because of *us* that this man can walk again. No! He has been healed by the power of God and through the name of his Son Jesus. Yes! The very same Jesus who you turned over to the authorities and had arrested, falsely tried and sentenced to death by crucifixion. Imagine! You killed the source of all life! But God raised Jesus from the grave and death – and now he lives! His healing power was released into the body of this disabled man – who now walks and praises God!

This is not just a story of healing but of access. What did you learn about this incident through the drama that struck you afresh? Should healing have been a prerequisite for going into the Temple to worship? (Compare with the invitation of the master to the great banquet in Luke 14.21.)

WWJD?

Did Jesus heal every sick or disabled person he met? Read and discuss John 5.2–15, where Jesus healed just one man at the pool of Bethesda, where 'many invalids' waited for the mysterious stirring of the water. Think about the likelihood that if the disabled man featured in the Acts 3 passage was begging at the entrance to the Temple courts every day, then Jesus himself was likely to have walked past him.

Digging deeper

Leviticus 21.16–23 prohibits priests who have impairments or disfigurements from serving in the worship rituals of the Tabernacle or Temple. How do we view these restrictions today? Referring to the Bible briefing notes, how do you think the events at the Temple leading up to and at the crucifixion of Jesus release churches from making similar prohibitions?

My story

In twos or threes, share any part of your life story which mirrors the experience of the man at the Beautiful Gate. Think about what healing looked like for Miles Hilton-Barber (page 65)? What might healing look like – if it's needed – for Clemmie and her family (page 66)? Can there be wholeness without healing?

Prayer

Solomon prayed: 'Give your servant therefore an understanding mind to govern your people, able to discern between good and evil; for who can govern this your great people?' (1 Kings 3.9). Pray for church leaders to have wisdom in reaching out to neglected groups in their communities.

6

Living with diversity

1 Corinthians 12.12–26; Romans 12.3–6

Purpose: to think about how to recognize and release the gifting of disabled people as a contribution to the unity and wholeness of the body of Christ.

Prayer

- Thank God that in Christ we are brothers and sisters, part of a local, a national and an international family.
- Ask God to give us a greater desire to find barrier-free fellowship with disabled people.

Bible briefing

For just as the body is one and has many members, and all the members of the body, though many, are one body, so it is with Christ. For in the one Spirit we were all baptized into one body – Jews or Greeks, slaves or free – and we were all made to drink of one Spirit.

Indeed, the body does not consist of one member but of many. If the foot were to say, 'Because I am not a hand, I do not belong to the body', that would not make it any less a part of the body. And if the ear were to say, 'Because I am not an eye, I do not belong to the body', that would not make it any less a part of the body. If the whole body were an eye, where would the hearing be? If the whole body were hearing, where would the sense of smell be? But as it is, God arranged the members in the body, each one of them, as he chose. If all were a single member, where would the body be? As it is, there are many members, yet one body. The eye cannot say to the hand, 'I have no need of you', nor again the head to the feet, 'I have no need of you.' On the contrary, the members of the body that seem to be weaker are indispensable, and those members of the body that we think less honourable we clothe with greater honour, and our less respectable members are treated with greater respect; whereas our more respectable members do not need this. But God has so arranged the body, giving the greater honour to the inferior member, that there may be no dissension within the body, but the members may have the same care for one another. If one member suffers, all suffer together with it; if one member is honoured, all rejoice together with it. (1 Corinthians 12.12–26)

I say to everyone among you not to think of yourself more highly than you ought to think, but to think with sober judgement, each according to the measure of faith that God has assigned. For as in one body we have many members, and not all the members have the same function, so we, who are many, are one body in Christ, and individually we are members one of another. We have gifts that differ according to the grace given to us. (Romans 12.3–6)

Bible briefing notes

In both 1 Corinthians 12 and Romans 12, Paul likens the church to a human body. Though made up of many parts of great diversity in form, function and appearance, all come together to make something integrated, complete and effective. The picture is one of interdependence, in which experiences – good and bad – are shared by all and faced together.

We tend to make snap judgements about people, sometimes on poor data and without proper consideration. If we miss out on the gifting that God has provided to our church because we don't see beyond a person's disability to his or her God-given talents, then we are in effect disabling that church.

A frequent mistake is to see disabled people only in terms of their disabling conditions and then assume that we know what they need. Disabled Christians who respond to an offer of prayer ministry often find that the assumption is made that their prayer need relates to their disability, that they are seeking prayer for healing. More often than not, the non-disabled person feels there must be pain and suffering in disability, whereas many who are disabled do not identify with those feelings. People who have a long-term experience of disability generally become pretty comfortable in their own skins. The challenges that lead them to seek prayer ministry are likely to be the same as those anyone faces: loss of job, money worries, relationship breakdown, whatever.

These passages of Scripture characterize the church as a community that shares its joys and sorrows, shares its resources and talents and fosters a wholesome interdependence. There's give and take. Some of us are serial givers and really don't know how to receive help. Some of us, perhaps because of a disabling condition, are seldom given the opportunity to give, and live a life of passive receiving. These are unhealthy imbalances in any community. There's grace in both giving and receiving and we need to cultivate both. Jesus said that it is more blessed to give than receive (Acts 20.35). Why should disabled people be denied that blessing?

Perhaps the time when we are most 'together' as a church is when we share in Communion or Eucharist. Sad then, if this is a time when, through disability, some feel at a disadvantage. But the way Jesus gave us to remember him can be beautifully multi-sensory and inclusive. With a little thought you can make Communion a richer sensory experience for disabled people.

The fragrance of a freshly baked or warmed loaf can fill the room. Breaking the loaf or wafer near a microphone can be heard as well as seen. Wine poured from as high as you dare is both visual and audible. We touch the bread and the cup. We taste the elements, with the aroma of the wine reaching our nostrils. All five senses can be engaged – so, celebrated thoughtfully, those with sensory loss can be engaged through their remaining senses.

The Disability Wall

Local churches need to demonstrate how God welcomes all. Church is the one place where societal divisions are completely irrelevant. A truly welcoming church would be a powerful witness in the world. We could talk about race or economic status, but a church for all – those with disabilities included – is radical. (Jonathan Lamb)

Saint Paul describes the Church as the body of Christ. It is the risen but crucified and wounded body of Christ, and just as the risen body of Jesus bore the marks of the nails, of impairment, so also must the Church if it is to be whole and complete in a broken world. The Church as Christ's body reminds us that all bodies are vulnerable. By accepting the brokenness of the Church we may learn to realize that the brokenness of disabled people may also be gifts. (Bob Brooke)

People with learning disabilities have been seen as somehow less than human and even, in some cultures, as having demonic origin! Often their disability has been assumed to be punishment for parental sins. And even where such demeaning attitudes have been absent, it has been thought that they either do not need salvation or are incapable of understanding enough to experience it. (David Potter)

The tyranny of normality . . . threatens us. The social experience of deaf people is more than just the fact that they can't hear; it's about the idea that all people must be the same. Deaf people who see Jesus, who want to respond to all he has done, who realize that he has saved them . . . then feel, 'Now I have to go to church.' And then it all just collapses because their experience of church isn't a good one, and that . . . means that their experience of the gospel might not be good – but the gospel is good for deaf people, yes? We need a form of community where we embrace and respect difference and diversity.

(Laurence Banks)

Real life: Paul and Edrie Mallard

Life was busy. Paul was the pastor of a church in Wiltshire and Edrie was caring for their family of young children. Both had a sense of calling by God and saw it as shared ministry, even though Edrie was a full-time homemaker and mother. Then, during her fourth pregnancy, Edrie became ill with a neurological disease affecting her mobility, coordination and speech.

Paul: I can remember going to the hospital the day the neurologist told me it was a long-term problem. I went home and was brushing the hair of our four-year-old little girl and she started crying and saying, 'Daddy, you're hurting me.' And I burst into tears. Men don't cry, but that day I just wanted my wife back the way she was. I couldn't understand how God had allowed it. I couldn't sleep that night, tossing and turning. Suddenly around 4 a.m. a Bible verse came to me from Psalm 18 (NIV): 'As for God, his way is perfect.'

What that said to me was, whatever's happening here, however tough it is, God is in control and he doesn't make mistakes. I shared it with Edrie the next day and we prayed that God would use the experience we were going through to be a blessing. 'Lord, we don't want to waste this,' we said. 'We don't want it to drive us away from you, we want it to drive us *to* you.'

I guess that's what it's proven to be over 18 years. God has used it in all sorts of ways to help other people. Not a week goes by when I'm not counselling people with tough problems and often they will say, 'Well, you understand this, don't you? You've been there. You know how it is to cope with things that are heartbreaking.' It's helped us to understand people and how God can be there in even the most painful circumstances.

Edrie: The Lord has trusted me with this illness . . . He knows me and thinks I can cope with it, so I am not going to let him down.

Paul: One of the things we've learned is that you can grieve deeply over the things that have gone – or you can rejoice in the things God has given. The whole of life is about losing things, especially as we get older. Loss has come to us more quickly, in our 30s and 40s, than to other people. This life is very, very short – like a mist. It seems so vivid and real, but it's quickly gone. Suffering makes you realize the wonder of heaven. It brings you to the point of realizing that this world is just the start – and the best is yet to be!

From interviews Paul and Edrie gave to Torch Trust's Insight *radio programme.*

Real life: Debbie Starling

It's estimated that around six million people in Britain are unpaid carers for an elderly relative, or a sick or disabled friend or family member.

Debbie Starling knows what that's like. Her first child, Gareth, was born with hydrocephalus. She went on to adopt Amy, who has severe learning disabilities and uses a wheelchair. And for a number of years she also had her elderly mother, who had dementia, living with them.

Debbie believes that loneliness is the biggest issue for carers.

When Gareth was born, old friends would keep away, even cross over the road rather than speak to me. Rumours go around, don't they? And things change in the telling.

We were led to believe that Gareth wouldn't develop but we ignored that. Seeing him respond to the way that we were encouraging his development was a joy. Every tiny step was something huge to celebrate. Now he lives independently and has married.

Much of the work you do as a carer – the round of hospital appointments, the routine things that take so much longer – can make you isolated. You feel as if you are in a battle all the time, fighting for the rights of the person you are caring for, whether that's allowances or extra support at school. And all that's tiring. Most carers would say that they are exhausted a lot of the time. If you are married then that can have an effect on your marriage, and many marriages break down if there are people with disability in the family.

Church has to wake up to the fact that everyone has abilities and we're all gifted by God. Many people in church still see things from society's point of view, thinking that the most successful and the wealthiest people are the most important. It takes a complete turnaround in your thinking to see vulnerable people as important and people through whom we experience God's grace.

From an interview Debbie gave to Torch Trust's Insight radio programme.

Questions for individual study or group discussion

Choose from this list:

- In her story, Debbie Starling (page 78) describes how friends crossed the road rather than speak to her after she gave birth to a disabled child. Why is it easier some-times for us to pretend that disability or deformity doesn't exist? What needs to change?

- Do you see a strange and fascinating irony in the fact that it may take the inclusion of disabled people to complete the wholeness of the body of Christ? How might this fit in with other things we know from the Bible about the way Christ builds his kingdom? Are there gifts buried within the congregation of your own church?

- In our individualistic society, how can Christians recapture the truth that 'we are members one of another' (Romans 12.5)?

- See Jonathan Lamb's comment on the Disability Wall (page 75). What dreams might you imagine towards the inclusion of marginalized people groups that might be described as 'radical'?

Taking it further

Choose from this list:

My story

Working in pairs, discuss what role in the body of Christ you are fulfilling at this time in your life. Or have you yet to identify where you 'fit'? Pray for one another.

Or

Increasing numbers of people spend a significant part of their week giving practical support or caring to family members who are disabled. Invite any of the group who are currently in this role to describe what they do. How do they feel about what they do? Refer to the experiences of Paul and Edrie Mallard (page 76) and Debbie Starling (page 78). What dreams might have been shattered when Paul had to take on the role of carer for Edrie? What ambitions might have been lost for the Starlings when their baby was born with severe disability? What have the carers in the group had to abandon to take on caring responsibilities? Pray for them.

In my locality

Identify people in your church doing vital but unglamorous jobs, perhaps as carers. How do you honour them?

Or

Are there ways in which you could celebrate diversity more in your church?

WWJD?

If Jesus had turned up at your service last Sunday morning, what clues would he have picked up about the congregation operating as the body of Christ?

Teamwork

Divide into two teams and give each team a 50-piece children's jigsaw, competing to see which team can assemble theirs first.

Afterwards, discuss the teamwork strategies adopted. Did someone take a natural lead, shouting out, 'Go for the edge pieces first; A and B, you separate them out while C and D fit them together...' Was there any confusion of people trying to fit the same piece? Did you get in each other's way? What level of co-operation was there?

How good is the teamwork in your church? How are people's strengths identified and used? Does it happen organically or is there a process?

Prayer

Say together this prayer, attributed to thirteenth-century Italian saint, Francis of Assisi.

> Lord, make me an instrument of your peace.
> Where there is hatred, let me sow love.
> Where there is injury, pardon.
> Where there is doubt, faith.
> Where there is despair, hope.
> Where there is darkness, light.
> Where there is sadness, joy.
> O Divine Master,
> grant that I may not so much seek to be
>   consoled, as to console;
> to be understood, as to understand;
> to be loved, as to love.
> For it is in giving that we receive.
> It is in pardoning that we are pardoned,
> and it is in dying that we are born to Eternal
>   Life.
> Amen.

7

Going to the great banquet

Luke 14.15–24; Matthew 28.16–20

Purpose: to look at the mission of the Church and how well we reach to the margins of our community.

Prayer

- Thank God that his eternal plan for the world extends to and includes each one of us as individuals.

- Ask God for personal assurance of a future life with him characterized by wholeness and perfect joy; and the desire that many others who are currently marginalized will know that same experience.

Bible briefing

One of the dinner guests . . . said to him, 'Blessed is anyone who will eat bread in the kingdom of God!' Then Jesus said to him, 'Someone gave a great dinner and invited many. At the time for the dinner he sent his slave to say to those who had been invited, "Come; for everything is ready now." But they all alike began to make excuses. The first said to him, "I have bought a piece of land, and I must go out and see it; please accept my apologies." Another said, "I have bought five yoke of oxen, and I am going to try them out; please accept my apologies." Another said, "I have just been married, and therefore I cannot come." So the slave returned and reported this to his master. Then the owner of the house became angry and said to his slave, "Go out at once into the streets and lanes of the town and bring in the poor, the crippled, the blind, and the lame." And the slave said, "Sir, what you ordered has been done, and there is still room." Then the master said to the slave, "Go out into the roads and lanes, and compel people to come in, so that my house may be filled. For I tell you, none of those who were invited will taste my dinner."'   (Luke 14.15–24)

Now the eleven disciples went to Galilee, to the mountain to which Jesus had directed them . . . Jesus came and said to them, 'All authority in heaven and on earth has been given to me. Go therefore and make disciples of all nations, baptizing them in the name of the Father and of the Son and of the Holy Spirit, and teaching them to obey everything that I have commanded you.'   (Matthew 28.16–20)

Bible briefing notes

We all like a party – well, most of us, anyway! Jesus tells a story of a great banquet to which the great and the good are invited. It's a big bash and there's space for them all. But the invited guests are more than decently late. The host – Jesus refers to him as 'the master' – sends his servants to remind them. Apparently, they have much better things to do.

Seeing the vacant places, the master acts in a quite extraordinary way. He sends his servant out into the streets to bring in poor and disabled people. In fact, a second mission to the streets is needed. There's no mistake here. The master's determination is that his house 'may be filled' (Luke 14.23). Instead of a party full of 'some-bodies', it's full of 'nobodies'. And notice – there's no mention of the disabled people being healed.

This is a banquet where those who are customarily left out get invited. It's not like most that I've attended, where guests are selected according to rank, or fame, or notoriety, or popularity. Usually, people who don't fit in or can't ever repay the favour don't get invited.

The message is clear. We have the role of the servants. Our master – the Lord Jesus – has given us the task of filling the seats for the party of all time. And there are still many vacant places at the table.

In the closing passage of Matthew's Gospel we find the Great Commission. Jesus musters all the authority he has – no one has greater – to deliver a call to action to his followers to 'make disciples of all nations'. The word 'nations' tends to lead us to see this as a call to mission activity in a country other than our own. But Jesus' words pre-date the modern concept of nation-state. The Greek word translated as 'nations' simply means 'people groups'. Looking globally, it's reckoned that disabled people – of whom there are over one billion out of the world population which tops seven billion this year – are among the least evangelized people groups.

Jesus proclaimed a gospel that's inclusive: the party invitation is an open one. Let's take care we don't make it exclusive to us and our friends, to 'our sort' of people. What are we doing to fulfil the mandate of Jesus, who at the outset of his ministry adopted words authored by Isaiah for his mission?

> The Spirit of the Lord is upon me,
> because he has anointed me
> to bring good news to the poor.
> He has sent me to proclaim release to the
>   captives
> and recovery of sight to the blind,

to let the oppressed go free,
to proclaim the year of the Lord's favour.

(Luke 4.18, 19)

Jesus states that his mission is to bring good news to people who are poor, captive, blind or oppressed. Though this can be understood in spiritual ways, we only have to look at the narrative of the Gospels to see that it was a very practical statement too. Jesus gave quality time and attention to those at the margins of society.

Even today disabled people can find themselves falling into all four of the categories that Jesus declared to be the target of his message: living in relative poverty, captive in their own homes, with debilitating conditions and oppressed by discrimination in community or workplace.

Isn't this something that as followers we should engage with?

Is not this the fast that I choose:
to loose the bonds of injustice,
to undo the thongs of the yoke,
to let the oppressed go free,
and to break every yoke?
Is it not to share your bread with the hungry,
and bring the homeless poor into your house;
when you see the naked, to cover them,
and not to hide yourself from your own kin?

(Isaiah 58.6–7)

The Disability Wall

If disabled people formed one nation, it would be the third largest in population after China and India: over a billion people. It would be the poorest, least educated, least employed, least evangelized, with the lowest church attendance. This is the mission challenge. Disabled people are not a distant nation – they are among us.   (Tony Phelps-Jones)

There are no steps into heaven! There are no barriers. Our access is gained through Christ. Not what I do, but through Christ and what he's done for me. Awesome! It's not dependent on whether we see, hear, whether we're mobile or not.   (John Naudé)

Death is no more than passing from one room into another. But there's a difference for me, you know. Because in that other room I shall be able to see.
(Helen Keller)

One of our greatest needs in today's Church is a sensitive awareness of the world around us. If we are true servants of Jesus Christ, we will keep our eyes open (as he did) to human need, and our ears cocked to pick up cries of anguish. And we will respond compassionately and constructively (as again he did) to people's pain.
(John Stott, in *The Contemporary Christian*, IVP, 1992)

Questions for individual study or group discussion

Choose from this list:

- How does the translation of 'all nations' in the Great Commission of Matthew 28 as 'all people groups' affect your view of mission?

- Read Tony Phelps-Jones' comment from the Disability Wall (page 86). Is this a fresh perspective on disability for you? What response might be required personally? From the local church?

- Does your church have a mission statement? How does it compare to the mission statement of Jesus (Luke 4.18–19)?
- Reflect together on the record of Jesus' life and ministry in the Gospels. Look at the balance of the time he spends with people who are power*less* and those who are power*ful*. As we seek to follow Jesus, how might this be reflected in the balance of our lives as individuals and as church communities?
- What do you think 'interdependence' might look like in practice in the life of your local church? You might like to look back at Gordon Temple's Introduction (page 1) to inform your discussion of this.

Taking it further

Choose from this list:

Discussion time

Eavesdrop on these various comments about the meaning of 'mission'.

- 'Preaching the gospel – that's the heart of it, and it's for everyone.'
- 'The mission focus of our church is overseas – mainly in the developing world. I guess that ought to include disabled people.'
- 'Mission is really all the events the local church does to spread the Good News, from the sermon on Sunday to the youth club epilogue.'
- 'Actually, everything the church does is mission, even down to letting the local over-60s club use the back hall.'

- 'The world isn't very understanding of disabled people and so the Church needs to welcome them and help them fit in.'
- 'Well, we might all be in their place one day . . . I want to treat disabled people with the same compassion and respect I hope might be shown to me.'
- 'Like everyone else, disabled people have something to offer the body of Christ – it's our responsibility to discover what that is.'
- 'Disabled people need to hear the same Good News as everyone else. How can we make that happen?'

Are there other comments you've heard and would like to add? Which of these are most persuasive on why we should reach out to disabled people?

My story

In pairs, talk about what you think has been the biggest barrier for you to understanding the gospel message. Then, as a group and using a flipchart, discuss the barriers (physical, emotional, psychological, intellectual) that might be faced by people with a range of different disabilities – Deaf people, blind people, wheelchair users, people with other physical disabilities, people with autism, people with epilepsy, people with cerebral palsy, people unable to speak, people with learning disabilities, people with mental health conditions. What would 'full access' to the life of the local church mean to each?

In my locality

Discuss the planning of a church outreach activity in such a way that it includes everyone and, in particular, uses the gifting of disabled people as well as reaching out to them.

Or

Remembering that the meaning of the Greek word *ekklesia*, usually translated 'church', is really 'a called-out assembly', how could your church find a meaningful role for disabled members? What problems might need to be overcome? Look at 'Holding an accessibility audit' (page 91). Is this something your church leadership could consider?

WWJD?

If Jesus was discussing how disabled people in your community are reached by your church, what three action points might emerge as a commitment to change? What practical outcomes might result from the time the group have spent considering disability?

Prayer

> Then Elisha prayed: 'O LORD, please open his eyes that he may see.' So the LORD opened the eyes of the servant, and he saw; the mountain was full of horses and chariots of fire all around Elisha.　　(2 Kings 6.17)

See Helen Keller's comment on the Disability Wall (page 87). Ask God to open your eyes to glimpse the reality of a banquet where everyone is invited and all together celebrate to the glory of God. Offer single-sentence prayers of thanks for that future hope!

Closing Communion

If it sits happily within the accepted practice of your church, celebrate Communion together informally as a closing acting of fellowship. See the comments in the Bible briefing notes for Session 6 (page 75) on how Communion can be celebrated more inclusively.

Holding an accessibility audit

There are a number of accessibility audits online which a church can use to check out barriers to access for disabled people. Detailed notes on this topic are not within the scope of this book, but some basic ideas are outlined here.

One of the best ways to ensure good access is to invite a disabled person to be involved in shaping church use and policies. There are many issues for discussion, and the selection below is by no means exhaustive.

- Is there ramped access for wheelchair users?
- Are regular checks carried out to ensure that the induction loop for hearing-aid users is working well?
- Are sound systems adequate and do speakers always use the microphone?
- Are welcomers ready to give appropriate support to disabled people?
- Are service sheets and newsletters available in giant print, Braille or audio for people with sight loss?
- How can people with sight loss or who are unable to read gain access to information that is only projected onto screens?
- Are projected words large and high contrast, without confusing pictures behind them?
- Is the lighting good and even – and flicker-free?
- Are directional signs easily understood by those who cannot read?
- Are sign language interpreters provided for Deaf people?
- If refurbishment is planned, have disabled people been consulted?

- Have disabled people been asked how they can be included in all aspects of church life?

- Is your church website accessible and does it have information that would help disabled people access the church premises and activities?

- Can you offer to email orders of service and song words in advance to people with sight loss or on the autistic spectrum?

- Do your practices surrounding worship, including celebrations of Communion, alienate disabled people or enhance their participation?

- Is the children's ministry fully accessible to children with disabilities?

- How are children with behavioural issues cared for, included and supported?

- How are the parents of disabled children and carers of disabled adults supported?

- Are your youth workers trained in the area of inclusion?

- How are you caring for elderly members with dementia?

Some of these questions may challenge long and dearly held traditions and need to be discussed sensitively. A key message from these studies is that disabled people should always be asked how best they can be included and involved.

Beyond the physical provision of the environment and the openness of its activities, does the church allow for the expression of talents and gifts which disabled people can offer to church life? Are disabled people able to take part and express their God-given gifting in all areas of ministry from welcoming at the door to providing refreshments, leading worship or prayers, church leadership, preaching and teaching, being active in the children's and youth ministry, taking part in outreach and so on? Does the church foster relationships of interdependency that include disabled people in a mutuality of giving and receiving?

Through the Roof offers a self-assessment resource for churches, entitled 'Removing Barriers', to measure how inclusive they are for disabled people; Through the Roof, ASNA and Torch Trust all offer training in disability awareness (for contact details see pages 97ff.).

From the Lausanne 2010 Cape Town Commitment – Part 2, Section IIB, 4

People with disabilities form one of the largest minority groups in the world, estimated to exceed 600 million. [The latest World Health Organization figures put this at over one billion.] The majority of these live in the least developed countries, and are among the poorest of the poor. Although physical or mental impairment is a part of their daily experience, most are also disabled by social attitudes, injustice and lack of access to resources. Serving people with disabilities does not stop with medical care or social provision; it involves fighting alongside them, those who care for them and their families, for inclusion and equality, both in society and in the Church. God calls us to mutual friendship, respect, love and justice.

1 Let us rise up as Christians worldwide to reject cultural stereotypes, for as the apostle Paul commented, 'we no longer regard anyone from a human point of view'. Made in the image of God, we all have gifts God can use in his service. We commit both to minister to people with disabilities, and to receive the ministry they have to give.

2 We encourage church and mission leaders to think not only of mission *among* those with a disability, but to recognize, affirm and facilitate the missional calling of believers with disabilities themselves as part of the body of Christ.

3 We are grieved that so many people with disabilities are told that their impairment is due to

personal sin, lack of faith or unwillingness to be healed. We deny that the Bible teaches this as a universal truth. Such false teaching is pastorally insensitive and spiritually disabling; it adds the burden of guilt and frustrated hopes to the other barriers that people with disabilities face.

4 We commit ourselves to make our churches places of inclusion and equality for people with disabilities and to stand alongside them in resisting prejudice and in advocating for their needs in wider society.

(Copyright © 2011 The Lausanne Movement)

Who's disabled? Disability in the UK

The Disability Discrimination Act (DDA) and the subsequent Equality Act 2010 both define a disabled person as someone who 'has a physical or mental impairment that has a substantial and long-term adverse effect on his or her ability to carry out normal day-to-day activities'. 'Substantial' is further defined as 'neither minor nor trivial'; 'long-term' as 'lasting more than a year'; and 'day-to-day activities' as things like 'eating, washing, walking and going shopping'. Faculties likely to be affected are listed as 'mobility, manual dexterity, speech, hearing, seeing and memory'. Also included are people deemed to be disabled by diagnosis of progressive illness, for example people with HIV, cancer and multiple sclerosis.

- There are an estimated ten million disabled people in Britain (out of a current total of around 63 million).
- Of all adults over the age of 50, 44 per cent have a disability.
- Every year 2 per cent of the working-age UK population become disabled.
- There are over 6.9 million disabled people of working age, representing 19 per cent of the working population.
- Of disabled people, 17 per cent were born with their disabilities.
- There are 770,000 disabled children under the age of 16 in the UK, equating to one child in 20.
- At 30 per cent, the poverty rate for disabled adults in the UK is twice that for non-disabled adults.

(Sources: The Papworth Trust; Employers' Forum on Disability; The Office for National Statistics; Contact a Family)

Churches for All

Churches for All is a partnership of UK Christian disability organizations. These partners have a breadth of experience and depth of knowledge on disability issues – challenging and enabling churches to fully include disabled people.

The aim of Churches for All is to help churches create and sustain an environment where disabled people can participate fully in church life for the benefit of all. Disabled people are involved in the leadership of Churches for All and many of its partner organizations.

The work of Churches for All is recognized by Churches Together in England, Faithworks and the Evangelical Alliance.

‹www.churchesforall.org.uk›

Churches for All Partners

Partners are Christian organizations that work with disability and/or disabled people as a primary activity, have UK-wide coverage and are pan- or non-denominational (in other words, not affiliated to one particular denomination).

Go Sign!

Go Sign! raises awareness of Deaf issues in the wider Christian community; uses British Sign Language to communicate Jesus in the Deaf community; and equips Deaf people with Christian resources in BSL.

‹www.deafchristian.org.uk›

Livability

Livability specializes in providing a range of flexible supported living services for people with physical disabilities, learning disabilities or profound or complex needs. The charity runs two colleges and an education centre for young people with profound and multiple learning difficulties; it also offers residential and nursing care for disabled people, and holidays for disabled people.

‹www.livability.org.uk›

Mind and Soul

Mind and Soul is a non-denominational organization exploring Christianity and mental health. Their vision is to provide quality resources informed by Christian theology and the latest scientific expertise; to initiate and facilitate local support networks involving local churches and mental health services; and to enable people to receive healing in a holistic way. Mind and Soul is a resource of Premier Christian Radio.

‹mindandsoul.info›

Open Ears

Open Ears is a Christian fellowship and charity for people who have impaired hearing and anyone else who is sympathetic to their special needs and problems. The main ministry is to deafened people who generally don't use sign language, although they also welcome BSL users.

‹openears.org.uk›

Premier Christian Radio

Premier Christian Radio broadcasts on MW 1305, 1332, 1413 in London, and nationally on DAB, Freeview Channel 725 and Sky Digital 0123. Premier is wholly owned by a charity, Premier Christian Media Trust, and is a member of the Evangelical Alliance.

‹www.premier.org.uk›

Prospects

Prospects is the lead Christian organization in the UK working with people with learning disabilities and their families. Prospects offers supported living, residential and day services, training, holidays and other events, resources and group support.

‹www.prospects.org.uk›

Through the Roof (TTR)

Through the Roof's vision is of a world where all people live interdependently, mutually giving and receiving, as God intended. TTR provides life-changing opportunities for disabled people and equips churches and organizations to fully include all those affected by disability.

‹www.throughtheroof.org›

Torch Trust

Torch Trust is a Christian organization with a worldwide vision for people with sight loss. Torch provides Christian resources in accessible formats (Braille, large print, audio), runs specialist holidays for blind people, supports over 100 fellowship groups for blind people around the UK, and works internationally, particularly in Africa.

‹torchtrust.org›

Churches for All Associates

Associates are Christian organizations which include work with disability and disabled people as at least part of their activities. They may not have UK-wide coverage; they may be linked to a particular denomination.

ASNA

ASNA (Adventist Special Needs Association) supports the spiritual, social, physical and emotional needs of people with disabilities and special needs and their families. It provides training, resources and breaks for carers.

‹www.asna.info›

Children Worldwide

The vision of Children Worldwide is to train, disciple and encourage children to be enthusiastic about starting and developing a personal relationship with God through Jesus, and enable them to become an effective part of the Church. To this end the organization works with churches, providing resources, teaching and training for children and children's workers.

‹www.childrenworldwide.co.uk›

Guild of Church Braillists

The Guild of Church Braillists advances the Christian faith by transcribing Christian literature into Braille – aiming both to increase the number of Christian books in the RNIB National Library Service and to supply material at the request of individuals or groups.

‹www.gocb.org›

New Wine

New Wine is a movement of churches working together to change the nation. Through a network of church leaders and summer conferences, training events and resources, the vision is to see Christians experiencing the joy of worshipping God, the freedom of following Jesus and the power of being filled with the Spirit.

‹www.new-wine.org›